Prai~~se~~

Musings
of an
Old Man

"The first pieces I read when our community's monthly newsletter and Writer's Quarterly come out are Dick's contributions. I never know whether I'll meet Dick the poet, the essayist, the philosopher, the humorist, the storyteller or a combination of these. What I do know is that I will find a relevant message for my life even when delivered in jest. The same is true for his recent books, *Once upon a Christmas* and *Life after Eighty*. As I read his works, I feel as though I'm in the middle of a conversation with a friend, and I look forward to the insight as well as the joy the conversation will provide."

–SUSAN R. MOORE

"Dick Smith's simple approach to subjects that are generally familiar to me has a great way of keeping things in perspective. His words make me more appreciative of my own life and values over the past eighty-five years."

–BILL MOORE

"All of those who share bittersweet memories of joys long past will find ourselves reveling in Dick Smith's refulgent poetry."

–JO WILLIAMS

"The prose and poetry of Dick Smith warms the heart and nourishes the soul. His words are a joy to read and reread."

–ROBERT LEONARD

"Dick tells it like it is, realistically presenting life's issues with which we are all confronted and in doing so helps us deal with reality, adding a touch of grace and humor."

–L. BARRY PHELPS, Assoc. Professor Emeritus The Pennsylvania State University

"Dick Smith, friend, neighbor and keen observer of things human. With his word processor, a pallet of everyday words and in Normal Rockwell style, he magically paints the every day things of life and how we humans react to them. In his poems, stories and observations, everyone can discover their friends, family and themselves."

–MATTY MATHESON, Bradenton, Fl

"For the past several years I have had the pleasant experience of reading delightful tales of life, much of it dealing with life as we age. These are the writings of Dick Smith, a neighbor of mine in our retirement community.

"Dick's writings have caused me to smile, laugh, consider the importance of what he has to say, and just say to Dick, 'Thanks pal, keep them coming.'"

–DOUGLAS DUNKLE

"Dick's writings touch spots that have been dormant for so long, we forgot we had them."

–EILEEN DUNKLE

"Once again, Dick tells stories and poems that take me to a treasured part of the past and relates them in a way that brings a chuckle, if not an outright laugh.

"Everyone over age 65 should read this book without stopping. Everyone with a parent, grandparent or friend over age 65 should read it. You can't turn the clock backwards, but you can make tomorrow better than today. Smith will give you some wonderful tips for easing into this thing call "old age" that we lucky ones share.

"Combining serious thought and wit, prose and poetry, future planning and memories, Dr. Smith gives us a peek into a well-lived life and a plan for continuing to enjoy that life."

–PHYLLIS DOUCETTE

"Richard J. Smith, Ph.D. (known affectionately to neighbors and friends as Dick) writes from his very BIG heart and shares a fascinating wealth of life experience.

"His use of well-formed English narrative and poetry written straight from his heart make every humorous anecdotes and partially-fictionalized "half-truths" believable to me (a Northeasterner). Each story is interesting, tantalizing, uplifting and meaningful. He captures you--whether or not you ever lived his or any Mid-Western prior life or have that sensibility--you get it anyway and thoroughly feel his warmth, smile, laugh, enjoy. If you are experiencing retirement in Florida or anywhere, you can appreciate his creative and poetic descriptors and uniquely clever perceptions of realistic challenges of aging or personal insights in dealing with those aging around you.

"I am a BIG fan, cherishing my copies of *Life After Eighty* and *Once Upon A Christmas*—I read, reread and share with family, friends and neighbors.

"Can't wait for each new publication!"

–CAROL LEE GILBERT, Westminster Point Pleasant, Bradenton, FL

"Witty, wise, and wonderful. Who would have thought that an 87-year-old author would have such a fresh view of life? Keep this book on your side table for times when you are sitting alone and wishing for a friend to "talk" with you about your world. You'll enjoy the good company."

–SUZANNE LAURION

Musings of an Old Man:

Some Prose and Poetry to Ponder

by Richard J. Smith, Ph.D.

ISBN 978-1-63393-595-2

Published by

 köehlerbooks™

210 60th Street
Virginia Beach, VA 23451
800-435-4811
www.koehlerbooks.com

Musings of an Old Man

some prose and poetry to ponder

Richard J. Smith, Ph.D.

VIRGINIA BEACH
CAPE CHARLES

Table Of Contents

Foreword

Richard (Dick) Smith's stories, essays, and poems have made our retirement community's newspaper, the *Echo*, a better publication than it has ever been in its thirty-three years. I was fortunate enough to be the editor of the paper and the *Writer's Quarterly* when he and his wife moved to the community and he wanted to write about his life here. And write he did! Just about every issue had an essay or poem about his observations on life in general, or about our community.

As a teacher of our language and a published author of many textbooks, his non-technical writings are a delightful mix of whimsy, "right-on" observations of the human condition, and good advice. It's in our DNA to think on the past. Some memories are sad, some bittersweet, some joyous, and all help us in our present to remember our past.

In this little book you have chosen to read, the author has put into words, in a way few of us can, thoughts and feelings we all have. He says it best in the poem "Memories"—that will introduce you to what his *Musings of an Old Man* has to say to you.

As I grow older, the closets in my mind overflow,

And memories spill out.

I lose names, dates, birthdays, faces, occasions—
many gone.

Those remaining memories I play and replay.

Some bring me comfort and happy thoughts.

I squeeze them dry with remembrance.

Others come on a wave of sadness and loneliness.

Why did I? Why didn't I? Why did it happen?

I must accept both the joy and the sorrow of my past,

As I must accept the joy and sorrow of my present
and future.

Life comprises both hills and valleys. We rise and
we fall.

We are all equipped with laughter and tears.

Life requires us to use them both.

My memories have taught me that.

Carole Sanders, Editor
Writer's Quarterly

Introduction

In a book I published several years ago, *Once Upon a Christmas,* I recalled that I have enjoyed writing for other people since third grade when Sister Germaine had me read my Christmas poem to the rest of the class. Some people don't care to write at all, but I always have. I enjoy good conversation, but I enjoy expressing myself on paper even more.

I did a lot of writing in my professional career as a university professor. Then, after twenty-some years of retirement, I shook off the dust and wrote two books that were well-received: *Life After Eighty* and *Once Upon a Christmas.* The positive reception of those two books inspired me to write *Musing of an Old Man.* The other trigger for *Musings* was the recent death of my wife, Jeannine, who for many decades inspired my work and fulfilled my life.

As a university professor I was writing for fame and fortune. In operational terms, that meant obtaining tenure, and promotions from assistant professor to associate professor to full professor with pay increases at each level. I taught at a publish-or-perish university. That meant write, write, write, or find a different job. So I wrote, wrote, wrote until I retired as a full professor, with a good salary and a pension. I had written and published everything I know. I was famous, tired, and didn't have anything else to say.

For twenty-three years I lived in a Florida condominium community where I lived comfortably, but without inspiration to publish anything. I encountered nothing interesting enough to me that I could make interesting to others. Then at the age of eighty-three I moved to the Westminster Retirement Community with Jeannine. There I found a culture to learn about and an audience eager to read what I wrote.

When Jeannine and I moved to the retirement community, she was still recovering from temporal arteritis, an inflammation of the temporal arteries. Her health prompted our move, along with a variety of other reasons. Our decision turned out to be wise and timely. Her health improved, and I came out of retirement and began writing again. I had discovered a population that liked to read, two publications eager for residents' writings, and an editor who knew good writing when she saw it and was not shy about noting on a rejected piece, *"You can do better than this."*

My musings consist of my experiences, and observations I have made about life in my eighty-seven years. The selections are both prose and poetry, all short and, hopefully, easy to read. They are biased, to be sure, because they are my personal opinions, thoughts, and feelings. Many of my musings—or most—are being reprinted, largely verbatim. The precise language in some may have been tweaked for clarity by my book editor, or to better fit this format.

My musings are varied. They range from the idiosyncrasies of the English language, to thoughts on growing old, to sentimental poetry, to observations of nature. Some are serious, some humorous and some sad. Those emotions are all part of life, at least as I have lived it. In this book I cover the waterfront of my philosophy, so to speak.

Musings is like a bowl of vegetable soup. Each selection is nourishing in itself, with the intention of leaving readers intellectually and emotionally satisfied.

The selections are humorous, serious, thought-provoking, and written with an economy of words, which is a craft I preached for years in the classroom.

Musings can be picked up and put down at any time. The short narratives, essays, and poetry all address the "everydays of life" we often fail to notice. They prompt both smiles and tears. Each offers something to think about and discuss with others. To paraphrase Francis Bacon (1561–1626), they are to be tasted, perhaps swallowed, and some are to be chewed and digested. All are to be enjoyed while giving the reader thoughts to ponder.

Finally, I'll leave you with a short story entitled "Lester" that implies our human condition is shared with many of God's creatures. We are born, we live, and we leave. The story is about how Jeannine and I parted with one of God's creatures, much as she and I parted years later, when it was her time to fly away.

PART ONE

A New Home

Conversations with dinner companions taught me that we older folks prefer the music we courted to over the music our grandchildren prefer. So I submitted an essay to the fussy editor of our community newspaper, the *Echo,* and she published it.

After slight success with my debut in the *Echo,* I submitted a couple poems and several other essays. No rejections. I was delighted. They all ended up in print. My essays and poems were well-received by the retirement community and my new editor. I was learning the kind of subject matter and working style she preferred for both the *Echo* and the *Writer's Quarterly,* a publication she had designed for the more serious writers in our retirement community.

I was also learning more about the subject matter preferences of the residents who read the material I submitted. In a conversation about something I had published or spoken about, someone asked about the use of "fewer" or "less" in the grocery store express checkout aisle. So I wrote, "How Many Items in Your Shopping Cart?" I earned a paycheck most of my professional life wordsmithing, so it felt natural to again splash in that pond. I wrote a few essays dissecting or debunking some of our most popular words.

One of the joys of living in apartment 402 at The Towers was watching the plethora of birds sailing past our windows and floating on the water below. Birds have an angelic presence and are comforting to the soul as well as pleasing to the eye. As beautiful as Florida birds are, I miss a noisy rascal from the forests of northern Wisconsin. I miss lying in a tent at night, both comforted and irritated by the night bird whose name reflects his song.

Old folks and high tech also became a theme of my musings. New gadgets are supposed to make life easier or more comfortable, but they often fall short of that promise. For me, and a plethora of men and women with waning hearing, eyesight, and mental acuity, gadgets can make matters worse. So, that became grist for the mill of my musings.

Suddenly, I was codifying what many of my retirement brothers and sisters were experiencing. They could relate and laugh at themselves through me. And I didn't mind being their foil.

Below are a smattering of the essays, rhymes, and poems I penned from my retirement perch. We'll start with essays and then ease into the more esoteric stuff.

First up is "Beep-Beep."

Maybe you haven't noticed, but you can't say nice things with your car horn anymore. Car manufacturers have been installing horns that won't let you express yourself through pleasant beeps or friendly toots with the tap of your finger or thumb. Now you really have to push hard to release a loud, harsh, angry "BLAAAT. GET OUT OF MY WAY!!"

The other day I tried to attract the attention of a neighbor walking my direction on the sidewalk with a friendly beep-beep ["Hi, there"] and scared her half to death.

BEEP-BEEP

We used to have a special "beep" vocabulary:

Beep, beep, beep, beep [The light has changed.]

Beep, beep, beep, beep, beep [May I please pass you?]

Beep, beep, beep, beep, beep, beep [I love the Green Bay Packers too.]

Beep! [Sorry!]

I think we could eliminate a lot of depression, heart attacks, strokes, fist-shakes and the need to carry concealed weapons in glove compartments by changing car horns. I would like to see a TV commercial by Ford, Chevrolet, Chrysler, or some other car company that proclaims, "Our horns beep." Soon all horns would beep again and the *BLAAATS* responsible for road rage and all kinds of other trouble would go the way of the manual clutch—they would have to be special ordered.

It seems writing, at least the way I taught it so many years, has also gone the way of the clutch. Technology has supplanted manually shifting gears of long-hand scribing, telephone conversations, or communications with beginnings, middles, and ends. That nostalgic feeling inspired the following.

I SURRENDER

It's over. We lost the war, and we didn't even know we were being attacked.

They sort of moved in, disguised, posing as friends, benefactors, *progress*! And now we are theirs. They don't belong to us. We belong to them! Victims of our own creations.

We don't write letters; we send emails, tweets, twitters, what next? We take pictures with telephones we keep in our pockets no matter where we are or where we go. "Excuse me, I have to answer this. It could be important." But it never is.

We panic when our computers "crash." Misplaced your cell phone? Can't find your iPad? "How can I live? Sound the alarm. *Help*!"

We are no longer ourselves. We are no more than extensions of our machines. Our children don't talk to us. They "text" us. We may or may not be on their "speed dials." It takes a year to learn how to drive our new cars without setting off an alarm of some kind. Soon our cars will be driving us. Cars without steering wheels? Who's in control here?

We should have seen them coming. Should have noticed when the typewriter disappeared, and a "word processor" took its place. Maybe that was the start of it all. Or when people started reading books on little gadgets. But how could we have known? We didn't see them coming. And now we're hooked.

WHERE'S THE CLUTCH?

I just bought a car, cheapest one on the lot, hand-crank windows, an engine, four tires, and that's about it. A simple key starts it, stops it, locks the doors, and unlocks the trunk. No keypads, combinations, just a few buttons to push, and no alarm bells. It takes me where I want to go just fine.

I traded in the most expensive vehicle on the lot that I bought a year ago. Lost lots of money on the deal, but I am happier than I have been for a year. I had that Super XRQ, or whatever it was called, for a year, and I still couldn't work most of what came with it whether you wanted it or not. It had dozens of buttons, bells and whistles, none of which paid any attention to me no matter how hard I pushed. I took a friend for a ride to show off our new "baby," and it started to rain. I pushed the wrong button, the passenger-side window opened, and my friend got soaked. I never drove it after that when rain was in the forecast because I kept forgetting how to work the mechanism for operating the twelve-speed windshield wipers.

When daylight saving time came along, I had to pay the neighbor kid twenty bucks to reset the clock, which also told the day of the week, inside and outside temperatures, the time of moonrise and sunset, and how many days before Christmas. Even the kid couldn't get them all back when they evaporated after he set the time.

The headlights were designed to stay on until I was in bed and had fallen asleep. I couldn't fall asleep wondering if the lights were still on, so I had to get home before time of sunset, which had disappeared from my clock. That was okay because I shouldn't drive at night anyway.

The radio did so many things it made me nervous to use it. So I bought a set of headphones and got the Oldies-Goldies station a lot easier. Once I pushed a button, and a woman's voice came out of nowhere to tell me I was headed in the wrong direction for Clancy's Pub, when I knew the shortcut I was taking would get me there faster.

The worst part was the door lock. Every time I closed the door it locked. I couldn't get back in without punching a certain combination of numbers and letters I couldn't remember. So I wrote it all down, but my fingertips were so big I kept pushing two numbers at a time and had to go back and start over. After three starts the whole damn thing shut off, thinking I was a thief trying to steal my own car. Finally, I just carried a piece of wood to stick in the door so it wouldn't shut until I got back. I had the car for a year, left the door ajar, and nobody ever stole it. But I figured somebody would sooner or later.

So I traded it in for a car a whole lot easier to control. Now I can lock and open the door with a key, and the headlights go out when I turn off the engine.

GIFT CARDS

If for any reason you are planning to give me a gift card to one of my favorite department stores or restaurants, please don't. I already have $14.12, $3.27, $9.23, and $6.31 remaining on cards from Macy's, Olympic Restaurant, Beall's, and JC Penney, respectively. I dare anyone to spend $3.27 exactly at any restaurant in town, or any town for that matter. Can't be done.

One birthday I went shopping at a Beall's "Senior Tuesday Sale" with a $50 gift card, and spent $59.23 after discounts on a gaudy plaid shirt and a package of Jockey briefs I had no use for—well maybe the Jockey briefs, but I later gave the shirt to Goodwill. I was trying to make it all come out even and failed.

Undaunted, the following Christmas I determined to match menu items to a $100 gift card at a fancy restaurant on the island. I took Jeannine with me because I knew that even at a fancy restaurant on the island I couldn't eat $100 worth of grub. The two of us used our combined math skills to leave the place "even-up," as we used to say in Wisconsin. Turns out we now have $2.18 remaining on a gift card to a fancy restaurant on the island. I'll sell it to anyone who wants it for a buck. Thanks, but no thanks.

STALE CRACKERS

When was it decided that consumers of certain products would be unable to purchase only the number needed? Take paper plates, for example. Last week Jeannine and I were invited to a picnic on the beach. We went to Publix to buy disposable plates, cups, glasses, knives, forks, and spoons. We needed two of each. Now we have fifty-three paper plates, thirty-three paper cups with handles that tear off when they are filled two drops over half, and more plastic knives, forks, and spoons than I feel like counting. They are stashed away somewhere we will be unable to locate should we ever get invited to a beach picnic again.

Same thing with socks and underwear. I had to buy packages of two-dozen each when Jeannine threw my old, comfortable ones away. I would have to change three times a day to wear that many out before I get some more for Christmas.

Our cupboard is filled with canned soup we rarely eat because canned soup gives us heartburn. We buy it only because some young executive at Progresso figured out that most of us can't resist "Two for One" or "Buy One, Get One Free." We buy even if we know that two cans of Chicken Gumbo with Sausage now cost the same as they did before we got one free.

I could rant on, but you get the idea. It's not just the money I spend for stuff I neither need nor want, but I have an awful time getting my purchases out of the impenetrable packages they come sealed in. And canned soup is no good without crackers—144 to a box with an expiration date.

SPEAK UP

About a year ago I began to notice I was answering most questions I was asked with another question—"HUH?"

Jeannine was the first to notice my diminishing capacity for distinguishing vowels from consonants in spoken discourse, and began telling me what to do instead of asking me what I would like to do. Then friends began snickering at irrelevant tidbits I interjected during conversations.

I knew one ear was better than the other, but I kept forgetting which side was better when trying to take the seat with my good ear next to the person most likely to have something interesting to say. I was living in a world only I inhabited.

Finally, a friend suggested I purchase hearing aids like his. I knew he paid a fortune for his and he couldn't hear a whole lot better with them plugged in than when they were in his shirt pocket. So he spent most of his time at the dinner table adjusting them or replacing the batteries. Nonetheless, I agreed to buy a pair and to see how they worked for me.

They were carefully disguised so that only my audiologist knew for sure if they were or were not plugged in. That's why my "former" friend in our poker group was sure I couldn't hear when he whispered to another player that I tended to do a lot of bluffing, which, it so happened, I was doing at that moment. I also experienced terrible pains in my temples whenever someone in our building burned the toast and the fire alarm went off. Once I sat in a group with an especially timid speaker and unnecessarily replaced perfectly good batteries.

But what finally drove me to be done with them was the discovery that the person I tried so desperately to get my good ear next to wasn't very interesting at all. So I dropped my new hearing aids off at Goodwill, having concluded that much of life is better seen than heard.

WHAT YOU DIDN'T SAY

Our language goes well beyond the spoken word. I have been told more with a smile or a scowl than by a spoken compliment or rebuke. Mothers are experts at imparting information with facial expressions. Fathers do better with sound. "Where in the devil do you think you're going?" All mothers need to do is look puzzled when you touch the door knob.

I nearly collided with another shopping cart coming around an aisle at Publix the other day. My near victim raised her eyebrows, dropped her jaw, and opened her eyes wide. Her expression said it all. "That was a close call!" I responded with tight lips and a backward step: "Sure was. My fault."

A day or so ago I stopped at a yellow traffic light when I could have sped through. In my rearview mirror I could see the driver of the car behind me drumming on his steering wheel, giving me dirty looks and perhaps wondering where he had stashed his concealed weapon. I wasn't about to return his dirty look. Instead I turned, put both hands in the air, cocked my head and shrugged my weak shoulders. "Sorry about that." He smiled, raised his eyebrows, and gave me a thumbs-up. What might have been a confrontation became a red-light friendship.

I have an entire arsenal of facial expressions and gestures. If you see me pull my eyebrows together, drop my shoulders, and sneer, you know I am not believing a word you are saying.

MUSIC AND ROMANCE

"Love and marriage, love and marriage, go together like a horse and carriage." That once was true of music and romance—no more, I fear. I can't tell much about the songs young people sing today because of the rate, pitch, and volume of their singing. You can add articulation to that list. But I strongly suspect their love songs are not as lovely as those our generation sang to foster boy-girl relationships.

Remember those love songs we all danced to cheek-to-cheek? Here are a few. Hum along with me.

"I know a little bit about a lot of things, but I don't know enough about you." Now those are lyrics that could start an engine.

"I'd like to get you on a slow boat to China." Remember that one?

Eddie Fisher singing, *"If I ever needed you, I need you now."* Are you still humming?

Rosemary Clooney, *"Come on-a my house. I'm gonna give you candy."*

"My heart cries for you, sighs for you." Can you still hum that one?

"Because of you there's a song in my heart." Tony Bennett.

"And when we get behind closed doors . . ." After marriage of course.

My all-time favorite is, *"I want some red roses* (sing it with me) *for a blue lady. Mister florist take my order, please. We had a silly quarrel the other day. Hope these pretty flowers chase the blues away."* What memories!

I think if our grandkids danced to more of that kind of music, their lives would be—what's the word I'm looking for?—*mellow.* That's it. Their lives would be more mellow.

Maybe colleges should require a course in "Music and Romance 101."

SHOPPING CART

Have you ever wondered why, in some stores, aisle one allows ten items or "fewer" and in other stores aisle one allows ten items or "less?"

I tried to explain the difference between "fewer" and "less," and why "fewer" is correct, to a local store manager and probably ruined his day. The sign in his store read "less." I'm sure the following explanation will satisfy your curiosity—if you happen to be even the least bit interested.

"Fewer" is preferred usage for items than can be counted. For example: grocery items in a cart, drops of liquid, trophies in a case, or dollars. "Less" is preferred usage for entities or quantities that cannot be counted. For example: food, medicine, success, or wealth. An athlete might have fewer trophies than another athlete, and, therefore, less success. You can count drops, but you can't count water. The fewer rain drops, the less water. The less wealthy you are, the fewer dollars you have to spend.

So there you have it, and I may have ruined your day too. The good thing about all this is that if you can count to ten, it really doesn't matter.

WORDS

As a writer, I am inclined to keep an ear on words, so to speak. And I regret to inform you that one of the most beautiful words in our language is ill. That word is *love*. Oh, yes, *love* is ailing from overuse. I would love to tell you otherwise, but otherwise is not the case.

Love has always stood high in the hierarchy of words. Check any volume of familiar quotations and you will find that *love* is prominent in the works of Shakespeare, Milton, Keats, and other authors of great poetry and prose. Ask almost anyone what word in the English language is most loved, and he or she is likely to say "love."

Unfortunately, *love* is now tossed around as if no more meaningful than *like*. Speakers are expressing love for objects undeserving of love. For example, a smartly-dressed female resident exited the elevator the other morning and was greeted by the words, "I love that dress." Now I ask you, does even a nicely-fitted, colorful cotton garment warrant the verb love? Or should love be reserved for a more powerful human emotion? What's wrong with, "That's a pretty dress."

I have said often that the Towers and Shores dining rooms are the best eating places in Bradenton, maybe Sarasota too, but I stop short of "loving" the meatloaf. It is high-quality ground beef, perfectly cooked, attractively presented, and professionally served to be sure. However, the feelings I have for my wife and children are not the same as those I have for a tasty chunk of meatloaf. I cannot love both!

One day last week I made a list of the objects speakers within earshot claimed to love. They ranged from pickled beets to "happy hour." (I could make an exception to my argument here.) Shopping at Wal-Mart, taking a bath instead of a shower, my doctor and my dentist, and having one's back scratched really are not love objects. Can a young man propose with the same word he used to describe the experience of eating a pepperoni pizza? I think not.

So I ask you, if you love the word *love* the way I love the word *love*, please use it sparingly. I would love to write more on the subject, but I have run out of space.

AIN'T SO

In the last issue of the *Echo*, I advocated taking it easy on the word *love*.

It's overused, I claimed, losing its punch, no longer emotionally charged. A number of readers agreed and told me so. Their agreement has given me the courage to take a position on another word, a position that may be unpopular and cause me to lose the favor I gained from my stance on *love*. But I am going to do it anyway.

What I am about to propose will likely come as a shock, so if you are standing, better sit before reading on. I propose giving acceptance, even respectability, to the perfectly good word—are you ready for this?—*Ain't*.

If you are still reading, I ask, why not pardon *ain't*? Who banned it from polite communication anyway? It is guilty of nothing. It is not pornographic, not insulting, not hard to understand. "I ain't going," says the same as "I am not going to go," in half as many words. We all like affirmation from our listeners as we are speaking. "Ain't so?" is less confrontational than "You agree, don't you?" or "Am I not correct?"

"We are all going, are we not?" seems stuffy compared to, "Ain't we all going?" Doesn't feel good on the tongue—at first. But neither does the first taste of spinach or your first martini.

Those of you who feel inclined to join me in this enterprise, to remove the chains from *ain't*, to set it free from word prison, to take advantage of its usefulness and economy of expression, do this: The next time you are served a tasty dish in the dining room and someone else at your table is served the same dish, say something like, "Ain't this good pea soup?" It may be embarrassing at first, but every movement has to start somewhere. Let me know how this works for you before I try it.

WHO CARES?

Pick any book on the history of the English language, and one of the first sentences in Chapter One will be something like this: "The English language is a changing language." We no longer talk like Shakespeare's characters. When is the last time you heard someone who changes her or his mind called "infirm of purpose" (Lady Macbeth)?

So I'm on a mission to simplify communication for speakers of English. Those of you who read my articles in the *Echo* know I have advocated liberating *ain't* and going easy on the word *love*. Now I want to put *whom* behind locked doors. My high school students in senior English couldn't keep *who* and *whom* straight, and *whom* was still being used incorrectly in doctoral dissertations I supervised. Making the distinction between who and whom is simply too difficult to bother with. And really, doesn't "Who are you going with?" sound better than "With whom are you going?"

Ah ha! I suspect some of you (if anyone is still reading) are saying, "Not I. I always use who and whom correctly." Well, let's see:

In which of the following sentences is the correct case for the pronoun used correctly?

a. I will give the prize to whoever chooses the correct pronoun.

b. I will give the prize to whomever chooses the correct pronoun.

(The answer is given at the end of this article). Don't look now!

My point is, who cares? Both communicate clearly. Let's do us all a favor and let the nominative case (*whoever*) work for both. Why go through the work of choosing? The message is the same with either pronoun. Do not be infirm of purpose. Stand with me on this. Let's let *whom* go the way of leisure suits for men and silk stockings with garters for women. We should no longer have to worry about that choice. Okay. Now you can see the answer to that test.

Whoever is the correct choice. It is the subject (therefore nominative case) for the clause that follows the preposition *to*. The entire clause is the object of the preposition *to*. As I said earlier: Who cares?

WHO'S THERE?

There was a knock on their door, and Tony called out, "Who's there?"

"It is I," came a voice from the other side.

"Who is it?" Tony's mother called.

"My English teacher," Tony answered without opening the door.

Tony's teacher was following the predicate nominative rule of proper grammar. The teacher may have been less grammatically correct but more true to the occasion by responding, "It's me."

Accomplished speakers are flexible in their usage and try to convey their messages without calling attention to their phrasing. No need to wear a tuxedo to Friday night Happy Hour at The Shores Pub.

"Who are you going with?" asks the same question as, "With whom are you going?" and sounds friendlier. "Bob is a better player than him," is as clear as "Bob is a better player than he." There is more than one way to skin a cat and more than one way to express a thought. Audience and occasion should determine the choice.

Our most accomplished television performers rarely say, "Everybody is entitled to her or his opinion." Instead, most say simply, "Everybody is entitled to their opinion." However, the former is more grammatically correct since *everybody* is a singular noun and *their* is a plural antecedent trying to act as a singular. Shame on *their*. "None are going" sounds better than "None is going," although the latter is more correct.

The goal is not to let (or is it "to not let"?) the form of the message interfere with the reception of the message. "I was so impressed with how he said it, I missed what he said." A good actress never lets her gestures overpower her lines. Conversational language should be comfortable to both the speaker and listener. So if someone asks, "Who wrote that article in the *Echo* about using words and stuff?" just tell them, "Oh, it was just him again."

I OR ME?

Some readers out there in *Echo*-land tell me they like my articles on English language usage. They may be few in number, but they are dedicated. So here's another "lesson" for them.

The conjunctions *as* and *than* are often misused because speakers mistake them for prepositions. Prepositions need an object. Conjunctions do not. Here's a little exercise to clarify:

1. The men I play pool with Saturday mornings at The Towers are better players than [I or Me?].
2. However, they don't write for the *Echo* as often as [I or Me?].

The answer to both items is *I* because the nominative case *I* is needed to connect with the nominative cases of *men* and *they*.

An easy test, if you want to be correct, is to finish your sentence:

1. The men I play pool with Saturday mornings at The Towers are better players than I am. (You wouldn't say, "me am.")
2. However, they don't write for the *Echo* as often as I do.

You can take the teacher out of the classroom, but you can't take the classroom out of the teacher. No one is a better example of that than I. (Or is it *me*? . . It is *I*).

OVERHEARD

"He's gotta be ten feet tall!"
"Really?"
"Yeah. Literally ten feet tall!"
Whoops!

The person in question is not *literally* ten feet tall. He is *figuratively* ten feet tall. *Literally* is frequently misused to make a strong point. *Literal* means *actual, exactly, no foolin'*. "I was so nervous at that pool tournament I was literally sweating buckets." I hope not. Nor was I *literally* shaking like a leaf.

It's okay to exaggerate to strengthen a description or assertion. It's just not okay to use the word *literally* to do it. It's okay to say that Dick Smith is *figuratively* the worst pool player in the world, but not *literally*. There must be someone on the planet who is worse than I am.

YOU BETCHA

Sometimes when I open a conversation with a stranger I am asked, "Where in Wisconsin are you from?" Apparently I speak *Wisconsinese*. I say things like, "So, how's by you?" and "You betcha!" I thought everybody talked like that until I set sail upon other states in our union.

When our granddaughter from Minneapolis enrolled at the University of Wisconsin in Madison, she asked me, "Grandpa! How does everyone know I'm from Minn-e-*so*-ta?" Her accent gave her away, even in a neighboring state.

I'm guessing you Southerners reading this think we Midwesterners don't know you are from the South by listening to you talk, but we do. You talk *Southese*. For example, you say things like *Y'all*, and you call people you don't even like *Sweety, Dear*, and *Precious*. And nobody from the South pronounces the *g* at the end of words that end in *ing*. "Y'all plannin' on goin' to the big dance, honey?" with a long sound given to the vowel *o*. If I talked like that when I was in high school or college in Wisconsin, I could have dated every cheerleader in the school. I played golf with a pal from Kentucky who reported his score as "faave." I tried to teach him how to say "five" with a long *i* sound, but he just said "faave" louder. Southerners also don't wait *for* something, they wait *on* something. I asked, "What are you all doing out here in the lobby?" I was informed they were all "waitin' on the dining room to open."

So there you have it. We are all idiosyncratic in the sounds and rhythms we use to express ourselves. I have now spoken both *Wisconsinese* and *Floridaese* for a long time, so I claim to be conversant in both. I like using *y'all* much better than *youse*. But the one Southern expression I have learned down in these parts I find most useful is "He's a no-good rascal—bless his heart."

VERY, VERY, MERRY MERRY

I am writing this in the hope you will read it before you send out your holiday greetings. Those of you who send them out early may already have included too many superlatives.

When I taught creative writing, I urged my students to avoid hyperbole and the adverb *very*. I instructed them that exaggeration will weaken your argument or your message. And please don't call everything you like "great." Having a *good* day is good enough. Great days aren't likely to happen, and people who don't have them will feel shortchanged if you wish them one and it doesn't happen. *Awesome* days are out of reach for most of us simple folk, so don't tell people like you and me to have one.

When the word *cool* came along to describe almost everything desirable, I thought it was, well . . . kinda cool. But I drew a line in the sand for *awesome*. Save that, I taught, for earthquakes or volcanic eruptions. There is no way anyone could live twenty-four awesome hours without acute organ failure.

Then the 2016 presidential election campaigns came along, and my mental red pencil got hot. I had never heard so many *awesome, stupendous, disastrous, amazing, unbelievable, deplorable, irreversible, unredeemable* adjectives, many preceded by *very*.

The election is tomorrow, so I don't know who will win, but I hope it is whoever used the adverb *very* the least number of times.

GRAMMAR HYGIENE

You may want to read this lying down—or is it laying down? Those of you who are not fans of my English language lessons may want to skip this article and send me a cease-and-desist email. Go ahead. I can take it!

However, I do get positive reinforcement from some *Echo* readers; so I persist in my efforts to promote good grammar hygiene. Some readers even like my little tests and have told me so. This article is for them, whoever (or is it whomever?) and wherever they are. Are you ready for this?

The infinitive *to lie* means "to recline." "*Lie* down and roll over, Spot." The infinitive *to lay* means "to place or put." "When you're finished rolling over, Spot, *lay* your bone at my feet." Poor old Spot. He is always being told to do something he doesn't want to do.

Now here's the tricky part. The past tense of *lie* is *lay*. Spot *lay* on his belly for almost two minutes before he decided to roll over. The past tense of *lay* is *laid*. Finally, Spot *laid* the bone down. Got it? Let's see. Choose the correct word in each of the sentences that follow. The answers are below the test, so no peeking until after you have made your choices.

1. Eventually, Spot's bone was [lying or laying] at my feet.
2. Spot enjoys [laying or lying] on the couch after doing his tricks.
3. Spot also likes to [lay or lie] in the sunshine next to the pool.
4. One day last week he [laid or lay] there until sun set.

5. Yesterday I [lay or laid] his bone by his nose while he was sleeping. He just [laid or lay] there until he woke up. Then guess what he did. He rolled over, picked up his bone and [laid or lay] it at my feet.

Good old Spot. What is it they say about old dogs? Ain't true.

The correct answers are: 1. Lying; 2. Lying; 3. Lie; 4. Lay; 5. Laid, lay, laid.

I wore out my welcome with that last one. So my editor suggested that I "lighten up!" I did that with some light poems. Enjoy! And I promise, no tests.

MY SCARY BOOK

Take a look inside this book
If you think you dare.
For in this book, this very book,
Scary things are there.

You'll meet a beast that's running loose.
It broke out of its cage,
And there's a monster in this book
On almost every page.

My poem about a wicked witch
Will surely make you shiver.
She catches little girls and boys
And makes them eat raw liver.

How about a creature who
Comes to your house one night,
And climbs right into bed with you
When you turn out the light?

I really cannot tell you more
Please put this on a shelf!
I've written down such terrible stuff
I've even scared myself.

IMAGING BY THE SEA

Sometimes I like to take a walk,
A stroll beside the sea.
Imagining I'm other things—
Things that aren't like me.

Imagining that I'm a wave,
Tickling this white beach.
Stretching water fingers out
As far as they will reach.

I make believe that I'm a shark,
The biggest ever seen.
Scaring fishes left and right!
I'm hungry. And I'm mean!

I might pretend that I'm a gull,
Resting on a piling.
Then flapping up above the waves,
Fishing while I'm flying.

I could be a great, big fish,
A dolphin with a snout.
Sewing up an ocean path
By dipping in and out.

Imagining I'm anything
That's part of this old sea,
Until a sand burr bites my toe.
And then I know I'm me.

LEFT THEN RIGHT, HEEL THEN TOE

Once upon a long time ago, Jeannine and I hiked every trail in the Porcupine Mountains, along the shore of Lake Superior, in the Upper Peninsula of Michigan. I would like to share this memory with you:

I hiked along Superior's shore,
Weary feet on forest floor.
The trail was sixteen miles long.
I walked and hummed a simple song:

Eleven miles, five to go.
"Left then right, heel then toe."

The world I'd left was far behind.
City things had left my mind.
No cars, no phones, no daily mail,
Just trusted boots against the trail.
"Left, then right, heel then toe.
Five short miles left to go."

Fallen trees were all around.
Summer winds had pushed them down.
"Left then right, heel then toe.
Five short miles left to go,
Left, then right, heel then toe.
Only five short miles left to go."

I heard a noise that stopped me short:
A breathy sound, a startled snort.
A bear surprised upon his tree.
His nap disturbed by noisy me.
My life depended on his whim.
To live or die was up to him.

He turned and ran. Afraid as I.
Why afraid? I know not why.
I'd like to hike that trail once more,
Feel unafraid in that sweet chore.
But there a black bear waits, I know,
For that song of "Heel, then toe."

BEHIND MY SMILE

If you think I'm never sad, I'll tell you what let's do.
You be me for just one day, and I'll in turn be you.
You just hop inside my shoes and be me for awhile.
Think my thoughts and do my jobs. Find out what
        makes me smile.
By the way, while you are me and one day passes by,
You'll also learn, behind my smile, I sometimes want to cry.

AUTUMN

Geese flying south
I'd watch if I could.
But with geese flying south,
I'd better chop wood.

Warm pumpkin pie—fall's in my mouth.
I can hear fall—geese flying south.
Trees with gold leaves—fall's in my eye.
The part I like best is—warm pumpkin pie.

MISS JOSIE'S PELICAN KEY BAR

If you happen to travel to Pelican Key,
Would you kindly carry a message for me?
Tell Josie's daughter I ain't comin' back.
I thought I would, but I kinda lost track
Of all the anchors hangin' on me,
Lost track of those anchors in Pelican Key.

You see, there's this bar in Pelican Key,
A bar that holds memories for a guy like me.
And Josie's daughter tends bar now and then,
But I can't go back there, never again.
'Cause I got anchors hangin' on me,
Anchors that keep me from Pelican Key.

I charmed that sweet darlin' with out-and-out lies,
Words meant only to light up her eyes.
But words that come easy to someone like me
Are not taken lightly in Pelican Key.
I got me a wife, a kid goin' to school.
Tell her she listened to words of a fool.

Tell Josie's daughter, tell her for me,
I can never come back to Pelican Key.
And when you're there, if she's still tendin' bar,
Would you kindly buy her a drink from afar?
Tell Josie's daughter to have one on me,
Have one on me in Pelican Key.

AN OLD FRIEND

A former neighbor and good friend stopped by yesterday.
We hadn't been together for three, maybe four, years.
He looked the same, but he was a widower now.
We spoke briefly and awkwardly of his loss.
Then we took up where we left off years ago.
We still agree on politics and religion.
We still disagree on less-important matters.
We drank a beer together, like old times.
He told an old joke, and I laughed.
As he left, I watched his familiar stride,
And I wasn't sure if nothing had changed,
Or everything had changed.

TO SOCIETY'S LITTLE WORKS OF ART

To seldom-praised necessities
Like faucets, nails, and front door keys
I offer our apologies.

We simply never pause to think
About the beauty of a sink.
And no one ever gives a speech
To honor common household bleach.

Oh what a pity, sad but true,
No songs are sung in praise of glue;
No poems immortalizing cans
Or forks or spoons or frying pans.

Now who has ever heard applause
For the sleigh of Santa Claus?
No flags are flown for hard cement;
To dental floss no knees are bent.

No parade goes marching by
Heralding the railroad tie.
Trumpets blare, but not for patches.
No bonfire's lit in praise of matches.
From wash machines to plain door knobs
You're always there to do your jobs.
To you who serve us night and day
From all of us I want to say,
You've earned a big HIP HIP HOORAY!

WHILE MOWING THE LAWN

A rustling sound, a small commotion
In the grass. I have a notion
It's a grass snake on its way,
To where or why I cannot say.
For I can't tell a grass snake's plan.
I only know the plans of man.
I've lived so long in city places,
Making money, reading faces,
That I've lost touch with things like snakes,
And deer and squirrels and bass in lakes.
A supermarket fills my needs.
I don't hunt game; I don't plant seeds.
I'm on a bridge that's growing longer;
My sense of loss is growing stronger.
I'm lonesome for the wild, I guess.
Why else to write a poem like this?

NIGHT SOLDIER

He takes his post at time of moon, while others take their nests.
His song is soothing to their sleep, heads tucked against
      their breasts.
He guards the fort while others sleep, this soldier of the night;
Singing out that "All is well" until the morning's light.
His throat must ache from so much song, he never slows his trill.
This sleepless bird, insomniac, this restless whip-poor-will.

PART TWO

A NEW LIFE

The transition from single-family living to a retirement community takes time. Although each person or each couple has a private apartment, they share much of their lives with others. Jeannine and I needed a retirement community because her memory was failing. We could no longer maintain our home, and we required the amenities and services Westminster offered. Neither of us expected to be happy living there, but we were. I wondered why.

After making some observations, and after numerous conversations with residents and staff, I was able to write the following articles. Several are assessments of the joys and challenges of transitioning. Thankfully, Jeannine and I had many more victories and smiles than defeats and tears, as you will see. I made many adjustments. As with Part I of *Musings*, this section finishes up with a few poems.

THE FIVE A'S

I am asked so frequently why Jeannine and I moved from single-family living to a retirement community that I looked back to examine the route we took. We didn't just wake up one morning and say, "Let's move to apartment 402 at Westminster Towers."

As I retraced our steps, I found that we passed through five stages, to all of which I have assigned a descriptor beginning with the letter *A*. As I queried other residents of Westminster community and those of another retirement community, it became clear that our transitional stages were not dissimilar to theirs. So I offer the following map many follow to move from single-family living to a Continuing Care Retirement Community (CCRC).

Stage 1. Anxiety. Most of the CCRC residents I spoke with experienced an anxiety-provoking event. It may have been a fall, an accident in the kitchen, or the diagnosis of an irreversible physical or cognitive condition. There was a reason to feel uneasy about our present living arrangements.

Stage 2. Acknowledgment. After a period of indecision and speculation, we admit we have a problem. However, we believe or hope it will resolve itself without major changes in lifestyle.

Stage 3. Acceptance. At this destination, we know we have a problem that is not going to resolve itself, and we cannot maintain our present lifestyle.

Stage 4. Action. We now search for the least disruptive accommodation for our abilities and needs. A number of avenues are open to us, from hiring home caregivers, to moving in with children, to buying into a CCRC. This stage is the most contentious and most likely to stress interpersonal relationships and family harmony.

Stage 5. Accommodation. We found our accommodation in apartment 402 at Westminster Towers. Others have found theirs in other places or in other ways, but life without movement from anxiety to accommodation is difficult and dangerous. No one lives happily in a state of anxiety.

This map I have offered may not fit all who are affected by illness or the aging process. However, it may be a good fit for many who are or will be in need of such a map. My hope is that all who follow it will find what Jeannine and I, along with others with whom I have spoken, have found: comfort and contentment.

WHY SO HAPPY?

Before I became a resident of Bradenton Westminster Retirement Community, I held a prejudicial expectation. It seemed reasonable to me that apartments housing older residents, some infirm, would necessarily also house a lot of unhappiness. To the contrary, happiness is much more prevalent among our community residents that unhappiness or discontent.

This phenomenon could be explained by any number of factors. For example, most residents could be happy because they are financially secure, have good educational backgrounds and family support, have secure religious beliefs, and are assisted by competent Westminster staff. However, it seemed to me there might be more at work here than the obvious. Consequently, I began a series of informal conversations and interviews to discover other possible reasons for the general feeling of well-being among residents.

From my informal conversations and interviews, I learned that our community is for the most part populated by adaptable people. Most of us have worked at a variety of jobs, lived in a variety of locations, traveled, and had other life experiences that require adaptability. Adaptable people have learned the inevitability of change and the necessity of adjusting to changing circumstances. Entering a continuing care retirement community gives adaptable people a feeling of comfort, not fearfulness or unwarranted suspicion. We did it before, and we can do it again. We are refreshed by a change in lifestyle. We are happy to be here.

My informal research uncovered other likely reasons for the overall happiness of our community. Chief among them is staff happiness. In an issue of the *Echo*, our executive director wrote of his happiness with his multi-faceted job here. Other staff members I visited were genuinely sincere about the enjoyment they derived from working with us to make our community a happy place. They are here because they enjoy working with an older population. We are glad they are here. We like each other. We share good vibes.

Finally, the residents with whom I spoke mentioned their appreciation of ready access to health care, feeling safe, having financial security, nutritious meals, entertaining activities, and educational opportunities. They sense that staff members respect them and have their best interests at heart. They have learned not to be fearful of an uncertain future.

The final piece of evidence supporting my thesis of overall happiness here came to me without my request. At the conclusion of a meeting of representatives from all seven floors of The Towers, a question was asked: "Does anyone have anything on her or his floor that needs attention?" One of the representatives from one of the floors answered, "Everyone on my floor seems happy." The other six residents echoed that observation for their floors. Perhaps not every one of our residents is *happy*. But I suspect those who are not are happier here than they would be somewhere else.

FORGET SOMETHING?

Shortly after Jeannine and I moved into The Towers, someone in a conversational group experienced a "senior moment." You all know what those are. The forgetful speaker, lost in mid-sentence, was spared embarrassment by a neighbor, who quipped, "That's why we're here."

We live in a continuing care retirement community designed and managed for residents past middle age. That means, with some exceptions, we are experiencing more and more senior moments. We can't run as we once could, nor can we lift and carry heavy objects. Our bodies have aged, and so have our cognitive capabilities. "I will never forget—old what's-his-name?"

Living in a community with people who understand and are not embarrassed by forgetfulness makes for more comfortable conversation. We don't need to be non-contributors in a group setting. We are not apologetic about our slower gaits, our hearing aids, our canes, and our walkers; and we need not be apologetic about our memory lapses. Like wisdom, they come with growing older.

Some of us have more serious memory issues than others. Those of us who are more seriously impaired may rely on support persons, who enable us to function successfully with others, and without a lot of supervision. Support persons can make lists of daily activities with us, help choose the right clothing for special events, make sure we take our pills on time, order for us in restaurants or the dining room, grocery shop with us, drive us where we need to go, remind us if we are being repetitive in our conversations, and on and on.

I like the term *support person*. It may be a euphemism, but so is *senior moment*. I like that too. Perhaps we should preserve the term *caregiver* for when we require more than a spouse or companion to help us out.

Names or terms that emerge from a medical diagnosis may be frightening or burdensome for a person to carry around. *Alzheimer's* is one of those terms. I avoid using it to label people with mild to moderate memory impairment.

Forgetfulness works fine for me, as does *memory problem*. They are more descriptive and less stigmatizing.

It is not surprising that a number of our residents give evidence of forgetfulness. We are an older group, and memory loss is a natural concomitant of the aging process. Few, if any, escape it. More than a few of us in independent living give evidence of our declining power on a daily basis. It is not unusual for me to be complimented on something I wrote by someone who does not remember the content, but remembers enjoying it. Even with a name like mine, I am periodically called something more complex than Dick Smith. We should call it a senior moment and laugh it off. Let's save the *Alzheimer's* label for the time we can't remember our own names.

CONCLUSIONS

As I write this, Jeannine and I have been members of the Westminster Retirement Community for a year and a day. We are no longer "that new couple." Those twelve months have been a pleasant learning experience. We both agree life at Westminster exceeds our expectations. We are well cared for in the present and well positioned for the future. Our decision to move here was a good one.

During the past year, I made some observations from talking with other residents, studying their behaviors, and assessing my own experiences and feelings. My conclusions may or not be similar to those of other residents on their one-year anniversaries. Similar or not, I hope they will be interesting to readers of the *Echo*. So here goes:

o   Upsizing is a lot easier than downsizing. We have all parted with possessions we valued, but which were no longer needed or didn't fit.

o   Feeling good about what you can do is a lot better than feeling bad about what you cannot do.

o   By and large, almost all people are pretty understanding and helpful.

o   Most people are going to be agreeable no matter where they live. A few people are going to be unhappy no matter where they live.

- o Westminster Administration either recruits staff members carefully or trains them well.

- o Nobody is going to be liked by everybody all of the time, but everybody seems to find a friend if he or she wants a friend.

- o It's good to begin life transitions while you are still able to complete them independently.

- o The eighties are more comfortable if you don't try to take too much of the seventies with you.

- o A free lunch and a tour don't tell you much about the character of a retirement community.

- o Attitude and a support group are essential for happiness at any age.

- o A warm touch is always welcome on a cold day.

So that's it for this year. We expect next year to be more of the same, and that would be just fine for us. We like it here.

MISSING A DREAM?

This is for all you dreamers out there. No, no, not those of you with soaring ambitions or high hopes, rather for you who sleep in a world different from the one you live in when you're awake. Take note: I may be having your dreams. If I am, you may be having mine.

I am convinced that what occupies my mind while asleep often has nothing to do with my life. This is pure speculation, of course, but I think dreams may be traveling from apartment to apartment. Last night I dreamed about my dog, and I don't have a dog. I had one long ago, but he was a different breed. So someone else's dog ended up in my dream, pretending to be mine. Is anyone out there missing a dream about your dog?

I dream about scary people I have never known and scary places I have never been. How can they be my dreams? Gotta be some neighbor's nightmare.

You could accuse me of making all this up, or even lunacy. But I have a friend on the fifth floor who dreamed he lived on the fourth floor and won the lottery. He hadn't even bought a lottery ticket, and woke up smiling. I live on the fourth floor and bought all kinds of lottery tickets. He had my dream, and I want it back.

JUST THINKING

The other day I read an article in *AARP Magazine*. There was a time when I didn't read it. The article was all about how to extend old age. A lot of young people are now writing articles and books telling us old folks how to live longer.

Well, this writer recommended spending more of our free time thinking. Just thinking, he thought, would give us more years to think. He didn't say how many more years or what to think about. So I decided to give it a try.

I sat in my easy chair, where I always sleep a couple of hours before I go to bed, and set myself to thinking. Well, I came up with the darndest thoughts:

1. There was a time I didn't say "There was a time" all the time.

2. I am either eating too much or shirt manufacturers are skimping on material between the buttons and the button holes.

3. I spent fifty-five consecutive years in school, either as a student or a teacher. When I turned sixty, the state of Wisconsin gave me a pardon and a pension.

4. Like a common cold, happiness and unhappiness are highly contagious anywhere people live in close proximity and have plenty of time to talk to each other.

5. Time is like smoke drifting out of a fireplace chimney. Now, if I put another log on the fire, I can't help but notice my woodpile is shrinking.

6. The number of people in either of our two dining rooms is directly correlated with the appeal of the first item on the menu.

7. Anyone who writes humor soon learns that not everybody laughs at the same thing.

My list would be a lot longer, but I fell asleep before I could think up an eighth one. The next time I sit down to add more time to my life I will have to find a different chair to sit in.

CAUGHT IN THE ACT

Well, it happened. My secret is out. I got caught in the act of make believe, a fool-myself behavior I acquired six years ago and that I thought would remain undiscovered. I was found out by a friend who unexpectedly stopped by one cocktail hour. Before you begin thinking I dress up in women's clothing or something even more bizarre, let me explain.

When I turned eighty, my doctor suggested that wine was a whole lot kinder to an old man's liver than gin. As a devoted martini drinker, I found that a most unpleasant piece of information. I hated to abandon my daily gin and dry vermouth in a special glass with an olive resting patiently at the bottom of the glass. So I improvised by substituting white wine for gin and vermouth—same glass, with an olive submerged in the new concoction. This became my daily drink of choice, and after six years I convinced myself I was still a martini drinker.

One afternoon when a friend stopped by, there was a full glass, untasted, waiting on the counter. I was across the room, too far away to snatch the glass from my friend, who said, "I'll take this one. You can mix yourself another." You can imagine the scene that ensued when the white wine hit a tongue eager for the taste of Bombay gin. By now all my friends probably know I am a faker who pretends every afternoon that white wine in a martini glass with an olive on the bottom is the real stuff.

So I confess. I am not the honest man you thought I was. Furthermore, should my doctor tell me red wine is better for me than white, I intend to put red wine in a fancy glass with a cherry and pretend I am enjoying an afternoon Manhattan.

STAY POSITIVE

"Acccentuate the positive . . . Eliminate the negative . . ."
Remember that old song?

Once upon a long time ago, I taught remedial reading to senior high school students who, for a variety of reasons, were unable to do what a lot of younger kids did easily. My approach with these students was to stress what they had accomplished after each instructional session, not what they failed to do. After they struggled through a six-word sentence I might say, "Very good. You said four words perfectly," not "You missed two words." There's a difference.

I think that principle is applicable to ourselves as we begin to experience the losses that come with the aging process. We are better served by accentuating the positive:

"I can hear a lot better with these hearing aids."

"I don't need a magnifying glass to read the menu."

"With this walker I no longer fear falling."

"Ice cream still tastes good."

"I got dressed all by myself again this morning."

"These raindrops on my bald head feel wonderful."

Now isn't that better than pouting because my hairline is receding? When I find myself feeling "Poor me," I make a list of "Still can do's!"

That always makes me feel better.

1948

It was Saturday afternoon.
We were eighteen years old, excited, bored, optimistic,
          fearful.
"What should we do?"
"How about a wiener roast?"
"Where?"
"Henes Park."
"We'll get the hot dogs."
"We'll bring the beer."

The moon rose over Green Bay.
We ate, we drank, we smooched.

It was Sunday morning.
We were still eighteen years old, still excited, still bored,
still optimistic, still fearful.

THROUGH THE DECADES

When we were in our teens, we had wiener roasts in the park.
Ate hot dogs, drank cold beer, and watched the moon go down.

When we were in our thirties, we put the kids to bed,
Ate pizza, drank wine, and watched the Johnny Carson Show.

When we were in our fifties, we drank cocktails,
Ate at a restaurant, and went to a movie or a concert.

When we were in our seventies, we stayed home,
Had a bowl of oatmeal for supper, and maybe called the kids.

Now in our eighties, we eat in the dining room, drink decaf
    coffee, go to bed early.
And are glad we are not out in some park eating hot dogs and
    drinking cold beer.

WE RIDE IN GOLF CARTS

We're from Westminster, we ride in golf carts,
With wind in our hair and youth in our hearts.
We know that you see us as we pass you by,
And we're happy to know that we catch your eye.

We may need our walkers; we may need our canes.
We may have some tremors, some aches and some pains.
But we also have wisdom, gained through the years.
We know how to laugh and how to shed tears.

We cherish each sunrise that brings a new day.
And watch the sunset, watch each fading ray.
We see you young people and remember our past.
We've learned what you will: that youth doesn't last.

You see, you'll grow older, lose some of your pep.
Your world will move slower and so will your step.
And when that time comes, as it surely will do,
Our Westminster carts will be waiting for you.

YEARS TO SPEND

A dilemma we all face as we near, reach, or pass the age of eighty is what to do with the time we have left. We have reached or outlived our life expectancies and have little predictive longevity data other than that of our parents. So the question that presents itself is this: What to do with the days, weeks, months, years, or perhaps decades we have left?

Some of us choose not to plan ahead because of the uncertainty of how much "ahead" we have left. Perhaps that is why some comment, "I plan my life a day at a time." Some of us are satisfied simply to awaken each morning, or, as old age becomes increasingly burdensome, we're disappointed we have to face another day. Some of us may be prepared and ready for death; others may be eager to see even one more sunrise or sunset.

We octogenarians have choices to make. Do we buy a new wardrobe or make do with the old? Do we take one more cruise? Do we fly to a family wedding or funeral, or send our best wishes or condolences in a card?

My observation is that the personality traits and instincts that have guided us in the past give us the most satisfactory answers. Our choices for the future are specific to each of us. We probably choose for our old age much as we did for our younger years. We remain the personalities we always were. What is appealing to one of us may be unappealing to another. We would be unwise to let others lead us in directions we don't want to go.

For example, I have friends who will go on a cruise regardless of the arrangements required or the possibility of falling or having to be airlifted off the ship after a stroke or heart attack— what will be will be. I have other friends who don't want to pack a suitcase or be far from a hospital anymore. Some of us decide not to drive at night or not to drive at all. Others drive a car until they are completely incapacitated or have their licenses taken from them.

Certainly capability is a factor in the decisions we make as to how we spend our remaining time, but so is mindset. Some people are determined to squeeze every bit of activity they have enjoyed in the past into their futures. They are more adventuresome than others. Some decide that lack of activity and adventure is more to their liking. It is a mistake to do what others do if you are not comfortable doing as they do. What pleases some folks displeases others, and that's the way it should be. Be true to your own instincts.

"Bon voyage! I'll see you when you get back."

PART THREE

THE HOLIDAYS

The December issue of the *Echo* and the *Writer's Quarterly* are Christmas editions. So, in keeping with the season, I submitted the following poems and short narratives. My editor published both poems and two of the narratives. But I include all of the narratives here because she and I thought they were good enough to be published, but space was limited. I guess that's why they make books.

The Christmas and New Year season is an enchanting time of the year, even when you're older. And the New Year rolls in faster with each year of age. These holidays change with time, but their spirits persevere. Tasks and traditions are passed from one generation to the next like a baton in a sprint relay. Once we pass that last baton, we oldies sit in the stands, tap our feet, and watch the race.

We start this section with a poem and we will finish with the same. Merry Christmas and Happy New Year!

THE WORDS OF CHRISTMAS

Speak softly. For it is Christmas,
And your words should fall
As snowflakes to the ground.

Speak words that comfort. For it is
Christmas, and your words should
Dress the wounds of those in pain.

Listen patiently to the sorrows of
Others. For it is Christmas, and
Those who sorrow need your ear.

Offer forgiveness to your offenders at
Christmas. For Christmas is a
Time to give the gift of peace.

Open your ears and mind to the
Beliefs of others at Christmas.
For an open mind is the doorway
To understanding.

Avoid bold assertions at Christmas,
For strident speech is displeasing to
The ear and disquieting to the soul.

Invite the reticent to speak.
For it is Christmas, and they too have
Words worth hearing.

Find and give the joy and love of
Christmas with tongue and ear.
For words are who we are
And how we pray.

THE STRANGER

It was obviously a case of mistaken identity. I told him I had never seen him before, yet he insisted that I had befriended him years ago in Cleveland. "Look," I said, "the only time I have been in the state of Ohio was for a football game in Columbus. Cleveland is as unfamiliar to me as Timbuktu."

"We were cellmates," he said. "Tossed in jail for some minor traffic offense. You called your lawyer and he got us both out. I was broke at the time, and you gave me a couple hundred bucks to get my life together. Never thought I'd see you again."

I insisted I was not the man he thought I was and vehemently denied ever being jailed, even for a minor traffic offense.

"I can see you've tried to forget the whole sorry business," he countered. "But now you're in a bit of a financial bind yourself, or you wouldn't be shopping here."

"Look," I said. "Why don't you just admit I am not the man you thought I was and move along? We're attracting a crowd. And I am not in a financial bind. I am an antique collector and often pick up a valuable piece in stores like this."

"Rubbish," he sneered. "You're the man I've been hoping to run into for years. I've been lucky with cards and the ponies, and I have a few other sidelines. I may be on the shady side, but I pay my debts. Take this, and no arguments." He thrust a handful of bills into my coat pocket and strode out of the store.

A small crowd of shoppers had gathered and taken in the unfortunate episode. "I'm sorry," I announced. "That man is a complete stranger to me. He may have been in jail in Cleveland, but I was not. Furthermore, I have no intention of keeping this money."

With that declaration I pulled the several hundred dollars out of my coat pocket. "He owed me nothing, and I am in no need of money." I paused. "This money I am leaving at the checkout counter with the instructions to take twenty dollars off each customer's bill until the money is gone." That said I left the store, stuffed a five dollar bill into the bell ringer's red kettle, and walked to my car. He was waiting inside the car. "What's our next stop?" I asked.

> For there are angels
> Who walk among us.
> Sometimes singly
> And sometimes in pairs.

CHRISTMAS PARTY

The tongue spoke: Listen, everybody. The eyes have
                         something to say."

The eyes observed: "We saw on the calendar that we are
                         all going to a Christmas party."

The ears reported: "We have been hearing Christmas
                         carols on the radio."

The heart thumped: "I'd better prepare for all that emotion
                         and commotion."

The stomach groaned: "But I'm still full from Thanksgiving."

The lungs sighed: "We had better get pumped for singing
                         Christmas carols. Thank
                         goodness we no longer have to contend
                         with cigarette smoke."

The blood gurgled: "I'll be carrying all that alcohol, sugar,
                         and fat."

The kidney and liver   "And we'll have to clean it all out."
complained:

The legs grumbled: "We will be expected to dance."

The feet flung back:	"Don't expect any sympathy from us."
The bladder requested:	"Well, please don't dance a polka if I'm full."
The brain commanded:	"Just a damn minute, all of you! Is not one of you happy about that Christmas party?"
The lips smiled.	"We are. Just think of all that mistletoe."

I MIGHTS

I don't make resolutions for the New Year. Never did. The words "I resolve" don't sound right coming from me. And the likelihood I will follow through is pretty slim. So, instead of resolutions, I will make some "I Mights."

For example, in 2018, I might "hypersupralize" my vocabulary, even if I have to make up some words to do it. My "farewells" are clearly undersized. I said "goodbye" to the young woman who bagged my groceries the other day, and she wished me a "totally awesome rest of the day." I was totally outspoken. I wanted to reply that in the previous twenty-four hours I had an awesome day and fell asleep before *Wheel of Fortune.* I believe I would be unable to get out of bed the morning after a "totally awesome" day.

I might also start using the word "impact" instead of "effect." (Or is it "affect?") That would be another hypersupralization. Used to be that impact was reserved for automobile collisions, plane crashes and other weighty bodies making unwanted contact. I recently read that what children eat for breakfast impacts their learning. Imagine what it does to their stomachs. I suppose in modern novels eyelashes flutter from the impact of a lover's kiss. Okay by me. I always did have trouble knowing the difference between affect and effect.

I might start inflating my own vocabulary New Year's Eve. At midnight I might wish everyone at the party a "Splendiforous New Year!" Then again, I might give the job to a designated speaker.

Here's another "I Might" for 2018. I might grow a beard. Beards itch, are a lot of trouble, and I look like a Barbary pirate in one; but I am sick of shaving. My first remembrance of that morning rite was watching Pa strop his straight razor on a leather strap. He kept a styptic pencil handy for good reason. Even at that young age I dreaded growing whiskers and having to scrape my face with that instrument of torture.

When I did grow enough facial fuzz to become a shaver, Pa gave me a safety razor with a new blade. I scraped a lot of skin off along with the fuzz and had to plaster little pieces of toilet paper all over my face until the bleeding stopped. Now I use an electric razor, but that's a pain in the face too, especially when it comes to brushing the whiskers out of the blade.

I might try to find a young, bright chemistry major and fund a scholarship to develop a whisker remover, call it "Whisk Off." If we can remove nail polish and varnish, why not whiskers? Just pour a little "Whisk Off" on a paper towel and wipe 'em off.

Better yet, I might fund a scholarship for a bright young pharmacy major to do research on a whisker control pill. We can control cholesterol, blood pressure, pregnancy and male potency with a pill. Why not facial hair? Then again, I wonder how many women would marry a man who didn't shave. And how many men would take the pill?

I might also take a few dancing lessons in 2018. When I came of dancing age in Marinette, the bands that played at the Silver Dome Saturday nights played mostly polkas and a few waltzes. I did okay with the polkas, but I never could get the hang of a waltz. So when the band played a waltz, I just danced the polka a whole lot slower. It worked pretty well with most girls who were used to dancing with boys who couldn't waltz any better than I could.

Then I fell in love and started going steady. That meant only one girl had to learn my two-geared polka. We got good enough on the dance floor so that years later we joined a dance club and drew a lot of attention when Melody Booth Band played *The*

Pennsylvania Polka, even though we were from Wisconsin. But times change.

More and more, our social set started taking cruises where instructors taught them to do salsas, rhumbas, sambas, tangos and other fancy, foreign steps I couldn't fit a polka into—fast or slow. So I found myself doing more watching than dancing.

It's come to the point that I just might go on a cruise and take a lesson or two. Unless—and this is just an idea—some bright, young engineer invents dancing shoes. Not shoes you dance in, but shoes that dance with you in them. Then, when Melody Booth plays a tango, you just set the dial on the shoes to TANGO and off you go. Of course, your partner would need a pair too, and you'd have to be darn sure you both had the same dial setting before you hit the dance floor.

If I follow through on my "I Mights" for 2018, I might be ready for a "fundelicious" New Year's Eve to ring in 2019. I'll wipe off my whiskers, put on my dancing shoes, head for the Moose Club and tango away the evening. Until then, I wish you all a totally Hypersupralized 2018! And a Happy New Year, too!

PRACTICAL COUPLE

He was a practical man. She knew that when she agreed to marry him after his proposal on their way out of the local Burger King.

"How's about we get married?" he proposed, standing upright.

"Why not?" she accepted, because she was a practical woman.

They drove low-mileage, used vans and rented until they had saved slightly more than was needed to secure a thirty-year mortgage on a three-bedroom ranch. They had two children, a boy and a girl, born at a practical interval. They had laddered certificates of deposit at a local bank and life insurance policies in amounts sufficient for practical burial ceremonies.

Their lovemaking, too, was practical. Once for each of the two children, of course, and on camping-trip vacations, some holidays, and the first Saturday of every month.

All in all, their marriage was solid, steady, and predictable. "We are practical people," they described themselves with some pride.

However, there was one exception to their practicality: their gifts to each other on Christmas morning. They carefully unwrapped jewelry, sports equipment, cosmetics, clothing—all top-shelf. And as each gift was taken from its wrapping they smiled with delight and exclaimed, "It's beautiful, just what I wanted. Shame on you. It's so impractical."

And every Christmas night, after their lovemaking, they lay next to each other in the darkness, silent until he spoke, as if on cue.

He: "Your gifts this year are great, totally awesome. I'll wear that sports jacket New Year's Eve. My old one is a little tight."

She: "And won't I look awesome New Year's Eve in that gold necklace."

Momentary silence, then:

He: "But . . ."

She: "But what, honey?"

He: "There's still lots of wear in my old jacket, and maybe it could be let out a little."

She: "I saved the receipt and asked if it could be returned if you didn't like it."

He: "Oh, I like it . . . a lot. But the tires on the van are showing a lot of wear. And we need a new battery."

She: "Did you save the receipt for that necklace?"

He: "Yeah, sure did. It's returnable. I checked that out."

She: "I really don't have the proper dress for it. I'll bet it would buy the best battery Sears sells, and a new garbage disposal too. Ours is making that clunking sound."

He: "And those new golf clubs are super, but I just had new grips put on my old clubs."

It was the same script they had used since their marriage. And why not? After all, they were practical people.

NEW NEIGHBOR

318 had been vacant only two days when Adelaide Murray moved in.

"Never thought I'd end up in a nursing home," she complained to her daughter. "And right before Christmas."

"Mother," her daughter corrected impatiently. "Fairview Acres is a living facility for the elderly. We don't need to discuss that again."

"Call it whatever suits you," her mother fired back. "It smells like a nursing home to me."

In truth, it did not.

With both doors ajar, 316 had no trouble eavesdropping on his new neighbor in 318. His neighbor of two days ago, Amos Buntley, no longer needed a room at Fairview Acres, or anywhere else for that matter. And rooms at Fairview never remained vacant long.

Fairview Acres staff often referred to residents by their room number rather than their names. 316 was occupied by Herbie Horvath. He had been a "happy camper," as he described himself, at Fairview for six years. He had never married, but had come close several times. Herbie had always liked a good time— with no strings attached.

Another cliché he lived by was "love 'em and leave 'em"— until he was the one being left and could no longer find women to love him. So, without female companionship, and being woefully inadequate in the kitchen, he traded fun for comfort and moved into 316. He enjoyed three good meals a day and the attention of an attractive physical therapist who moved his limbs in a variety of directions to ease his stiff muscles and arthritic joints. Lying on her bench, listening to her litanies of boyfriend troubles, Herbie was titillated by memories of the good old days.

Now he was listening to the daughter of his next door neighbor bid her apprehensive mother goodbye.

"Do try to be happy here, Mother. You'll make friends with other women who play bridge, and you won't have to cook or clean house or worry about anything. Take a nap now in this lovely room. And I'll pick you up Christmas morning for the whole day at our house."

Adelaide Murray was a longtime widow. When people asked her how long she had been a widow, she had a hard time remembering.

"Why, Art's been gone ten . . . let me see . . . has he been gone fourteen years already?"

So it had been fourteen years, and some time before that, since she had loved and been loved by a man. Nonetheless, she kept up her appearance with weekly appointments at a good salon. Not that she wanted another man, but she enjoyed being told she looked so much younger than her age and, well, you never know.

Room 316 watched for 318 in the community room, at the jigsaw puzzle table and in the dining room; but there were no new faces at any of these. He concluded 318 must be taking her meals in her room for forty bucks a month more. And he also concluded she must be getting lonely, it being the Christmas season and all. So, after the Christmas Eve dinner, and after the carolers left, Herbie made a bold move. Instead of turning into 316, he took a few more steps, thought for a moment, then tapped gently on the half-opened door of 318. He waited and tapped again, not so gently. Then he heard a teary voice, "Go away, I've had my dinner."

"That you, Amos?"

"Who?"

"Amos!"

"Amos doesn't live here anymore."

"Well, I'll be dammed. Who does live here?"

"Mrs. Adelaide Murray. I mean, I do, for now."

"Well, Mrs. Adelaide Murray, since we're neighbors and all, I'd like to wish my new neighbor a Merry Christmas."

Long silence.

"How about it, Mrs. Murray? How's about I stick my head in, just to wish my new neighbor a Merry Christmas and all?"

Shorter silence.

"Well, if you don't stay long. My daughter will be calling for me very early in the morning."

"Don't take long for me to say, 'Merry Christmas,' Mrs. Murray."

"Come in then, but for just a moment."

Herbie had never had acting lessons, but the startled pose he struck as he entered 318 would have won him an Oscar.

Herbie: "Sorry, but I thought you said it was you living here . . . for now, I mean.

Adelaide: "I am unless I choose to return home. And why does that surprise you, Mr. . . . ?"

Herbie: "Horvath, Herbert Horvath. And I'm surprised because you are much too young to be living next door to an old coot like me. Merry Christmas, pretty neighbor. And I'm wishing I had a sprig of mistletoe to hold over that lovely hairdo, Mrs. Murray."

Herbie's flirtation resurrected the tingle in her toes Adelaide hadn't felt since she was a cheerleader at the University of Wisconsin and Bucky Badger kissed her under the bleachers at Camp Randall after the Ohio State game. She felt her cheeks grow warmer.

"Please, call me Adelaide, or just Addy."

"Addy it is. And how about calling me just Herbie?"

Instincts Herbie thought were gone forever raised his blood pressure well past 120/80. He pressed his attack.

"I'm thinking, Addy," he said as his eyes captured hers, "that this being Christmas Eve and all, and both of us needing to get to know our next-door neighbor and all, why, maybe you'd be willing to join me in a glass of Christmas cheer and a few Christmas carols on my radio next door."

Adelaide, toes tingling and cheeks warming, rose from her chair. And from a distant somewhere in the past she remembered the words of temptation and submission:

"Why, Herbie, I'd be pleased to join you in a sip of Christmas cheer and a few carols, but just a few, mind you. My daughter is calling for me early tomorrow morning."

It was a good thing the Fairview Acres morning nurse checked out room 316 before 318, or she would have reported 318 missing on Christmas morning.

NEW YEAR'S EVE 2015

I hear a voice: "Stop. You go too fast.
My old pants have no patches,
Yet you dress me in new.

Slow down! There are things undone—
Matters still to be tidied up.
Go back. I am not ready for new.

Hold on awhile longer. Please?
My time is growing shorter.
How many more of anything do I have?

A new year? Why?
I am not yet finished with the old.
Why leave it so soon?" The voice is mine.

NIGHT THOUGHTS

Sometimes, awake in the darkness of the night,
I am attacked by thoughts of all that has gone by me.
Over, under me, through me.
Thoughts released at night from the closets of my memory.
Thoughts that disturb my peace and disrupt my sleep.

The years scroll back, and I am perplexed.
Surely these scenes and sounds belong to someone else.
Was it I who did this, said this, heard this?
Hard to reconcile, for I am not now who I was.
Yet I know it was I. Who else?

What would I do differently, say differently, hear differently?
Too late for different—what's done, is done.
Then what would I, in hindsight, repeat?
What do the same, say the same, hear the same?
What be comforted by in future dark nights?

Then with clarity a consoling thought:
Still time for repetition. Still time
To do, say, hear the stuff of thoughts
That will comfort me in the darkness of nights to come.
The closet doors close, and I am rescued by sleep.

THE PICTURES ON MY DESK

The oldest was six, maybe seven.
Her twin sisters were five, maybe six.
Heads touching, they smiled at my camera,
Big smiles that revealed spaces where baby teeth had been.
We had been rough-housing. All three against me.
I surrendered and took their picture.
They were exhausted, happy, triumphant!
They look at me now from that picture on my desk.
Grandmothers now, but still little girls.
They still want my approval, still laugh at my antics.
I still want to please them, see them happy and triumphant.
It's only a picture, but for me it giggles.

HEY, BUDDY!

I spent a moment with an old friend last night.
He's been dead for ten plus years.
I hadn't thought of him for seven, maybe more.
But it was Charlie, okay. I know it was.
My dreams tend to be repetitious, same-old, same-old.
I am lost. I am falling. I can fly. I'm in love.
But last night was different. Charlie was back.

Charlie and I shared a lot.
We were both pals and friends. There's a difference.
Friends can "unload."
Pals laugh a lot and slap each other on the back.
Friends trust and help each other. They don't compete.

It was a dream with a good ending.
I was in a parking ramp, in a hurry, late for something.
I couldn't find my car and ran from level to level.
Then I heard a voice and saw a silhouette.
"It's over here, buddy."

PART FOUR

GOODBYE AND HELLO

When Jeannine and I moved from our summer home in Wisconsin and our winter home in Florida to Westminster Retirement Community, our lifestyles changed significantly. We left a lot behind, which inspired this poem.

I've left a lot behind me.
Can't say I miss it much.
Most of it was trouble,
Houses, yards, and such.

Now I'm living simply,
Have only what I need.
My books, my bed, an easy chair.
Enough to eat and read.

Don't worry 'bout the plumbing,
A house that needs some paint,

A lawn in need of mowing,
Complaint upon complaint.

I'm settled pretty nicely,
An apartment meets my needs.
I'm now a man of leisure,
A man who sits and reads.

In truth, the poem expresses Jeannine's feelings more than mine at the time of the move. Now I feel as she did then.

Jeannine's progressing dementia required a smaller world for her. The large world we had lived in for sixty-four years became increasingly confusing for her, and I couldn't give her the care and comfort she required. At Westminster we had a much smaller world that required very little from each of us. Our meals, housekeeping, and social activities were all provided for us. She was happy, and I was not unhappy.

Her physical health, appetite, sleep habits, and attitude improved. Staff and neighbors knew all about fading memories, acknowledged and accommodated for folks who had them. To forget names, places, and past events was not uncommon at Westminster, where there was little need to remember the past. We were all in this time called *old age* together. We had an excellent memory-care unit, but none of us looked forward to the day we or a loved one needed to move there. For Jeannine that day never arrived.

I drove Jeannine to our family physician for her semi-annual checkup. She was in excellent condition with the exception of a suspected urinary tract infection.

Further testing indicated the UTI was an incorrect diagnosis. The correct diagnosis was stomach cancer. She died three months after that discovery.

Westminster staff and residents rescued me from the devastating grief that consumed me. Many had been where I was. I knew then what others knew before it was my turn to know. I now shouldered the heavy burden of grief that comes with losing a spouse, a burden one of all but a very few married couples will carry.

YESTERDAY, TODAY, TOMORROW

I have led an active life. My list of "Things To Do" has always been longer than my list of "Missions Accomplished." So I never got around to the photo albums I was going to get around to someday.

Well, yesterday was that "someday." I found and pulled an album from its storage place and began turning pages. Ma and Pa, now dead almost fifteen years, were there; and my deceased brother, who was eleven years younger than I. Other relatives, friends, places I haven't seen or thought about for a long time were there. And a young Jeannine, of course, wearing that smile all who knew her remember her by.

There were pictures of our daughters in their cribs and in their First Communion dresses; our son riding his first bicycle. They are all retired now with grandchildren of their own. Is it possible they and I have grown so old? Seems like yesterday.

None of those pictured in that album are as they were when those pictures were taken. Nor am I. Our todays become our yesterdays faster than we anticipated. But our yesterdays are real and can never be taken from us. Erasers don't work on what was once ours. Someday I will be a photo in someone's collection, probably in an electronic storage unit of some kind, and be remembered.

I won't be gone in the tomorrows that come after me. I will be in the yesterdays.

And the circle will remain unbroken.

ANGELS AMONG US

The images of angels most of us cherish are those depicted by early artists. In those paintings, angels have wings, strum harps, wear white gowns, and sit on clouds. But I have walked with angels who have none of those characteristics. Those I have seen are dressed as you and I dress when we act to bring comfort to those among us in need. The angels who ministered to me wrote notes, sent cards, shook hands, spoke a kind word, gave hugs, and in a dozen different ways offered sympathy and assistance to a grieving friend.

Angels walk on the ground in regular clothing. They eat with us, play cards and pool with us, invite us to talk, allow us to cry, and some even share a pitcher of beer with us on Saturday afternoons.

I live in a home with angels who don't look at all like those on the walls of art galleries all over the world. They look like ministers of all faiths, the nurses, physicians, and aides in health centers. They look like the administrative staff here, the dining room supervisors, cooks, and servers. They look like our housekeepers, maintenance workers, and receptionists. And the residents from all three buildings. I haven't listed them all, but I have walked with them and received their many kindnesses.

Angels walk among us and touch us when we need a touch. Thank you.

A NEW NOW

We look before and after,
And pine for what is not;
Our sincerest laughter
With some pain is fraught;
Our sweetest songs are those
That tell of saddest thoughts.

—Percy Bysshe Shelley (1792-1822)

I taught those lines to high school seniors, most of whom had yet to experience the commingling of joy and sadness older folks know well.

"I laughed so hard I cried." A familiar revelation. Tears and laughter are often not far apart. We are creatures who encounter happiness and sorrow at all stages of our lives. A baby's tears are turned to a smile by a mother's kiss. Young lovers part and reunite. Married couples quarrel and make up. Sooner or later death robs us of a relationship we hoped would last forever.

And so it is. All through our lives we hitch up our pants and go on. We search for an answer to our ups and downs and make do with what we have left after the downs. Wisdom comes from learning that going on is what we are meant to do.

I write these lines knowing that Shelley's poem will be more meaningful to you than it was for my high school seniors. But that was a long time ago; I hope as they grew older, they understood.

I wrote in a poem published earlier, "Our now is not forever." And when death takes away a relationship, "We walk without movement and talk without sound." But with help we search for and find new nows. Our talk returns to sound and we walk again with movement. When we think we can't go on, we do. And in time we touch happiness again. Those of us who have been there help those who are arriving. We thought we would never recover, but somehow, with help, we do.

My thanks to all who have helped in my recovery and are helping me to find a new now.

SHADOWS

Last night I tried to remember:
What you looked like,
How you laughed,
Your smile,
Your leaving.
And I couldn't.
That makes me sad,
For you loved me, and I loved you.
Now the love remains, but neither you nor I.
I am no longer who I was. I am a memory of me
And you are gone . . . A memory also.
I walk without movement;
I talk without sound.
I sleep with memories.
You must also.
For what once was will always be.
Now there are shadows where lovers once lay.

SMOKE

My time has taken on a new reality.
Now months, decades, years drift away
Like smoke from a fireplace chimney.
I put another log on the fire,
And am aware of my dwindling woodpile.

Who now lives in the house I sold too cheaply?
Who drives the car I traded for new?
Who wears the winter jacket I gave to Goodwill?
The lilac bushes alongside the back porch
Are they in bloom?

These and other questions join the rising smoke.

Do my memories bring me sadness? Elicit tears?
I answer, "No. They bring me comfort."
For my memories now return me to the house
I felt at home in.

I can still drive the car I sold, wear that warm
And cozy jacket,
Smell the lilacs in the smoldering wood.

But there is no smoldering wood.
No fireplace. No smoke drifting from a chimney.
Those are memories also.
So I will put another log on the fire
And maybe sleep awhile.

LEAVES FROM TREES

The pages drop from calendars
Like leaves from trees in the autumn winds.
Where does the time go?
Can it be June already?
What happened to April and May?
I awaken in the morning,
And it is too soon time for bed.
I thought as I grew older
Time would grow heavy on my hands.
But months are now shorter,
And days have fewer hours.
I have fewer things to do now,
But it takes longer for me to do them.
I stay busy with less to do.
Who knew that our older years
Would pass more quickly than our younger?
Perhaps God planned as we grow closer to Him,
Our waiting time grows shorter.

TRAILING CLOUDS

I have been reviewing some of the literature I was taught when I was much too young to understand and appreciate it. I am now able both to understand and appreciate an ode by English poet William Wordsworth (1770–1850), and I would like to share the following lines with you.

> Our birth is but a sleep and a forgetting;
> The soul that rises with us, our life's star,
> Hath elsewhere its setting
> And cometh from afar;
> Not in entire forgetfulness,
> And not in utter nakedness,
> But trailing clouds of glory do we come
> From God, Who is our home.

These lines are a comforting explanation of the meaning of life. The time we spend on this earth is only an interlude. We are music that emanates from a composer and returns to that composer. We sing, we dance; we fuss and we fret. We laugh and we cry. We are born, and we die.

Through it all we feel the tug from our genesis, the itch we cannot scratch—our feeling that our home is not here. We long for our beginning, the *elsewhere* our life's star began. The clouds of glory from the place we left cling to us to remind us, in good times and bad, that this life is but a sleep and a forgetting, not the home from whence we came and will return.

WHY THIS MORNING

This morning I awakened in a mist of sadness,
Perhaps the remnant of a bad dream.
I searched for an explanation:
An illness, a death, some other grave misfortune?
Maybe the memory of some forgotten event.
If so, why this morning when all is well?
Was it a premonition of grief to come?
Why was I in the grip of sadness?
It is noon, and the mist is nearly gone.
The sun is bright, the clouds are fluffy, another pleasant day.
I am engaged in my daily routine, as planned. Nothing amiss.
Yet some disturbing sadness clings like a cobweb.
Happily, it is disappearing; and I am being restored.
Soon I will be myself again. Self-assured, confident in the future.
Could it be that God interrupts our happiness now and then
To remind us that our "now" is not forever?

A DIFFERENT TRAIL

Recently, I was disconnected from life by the death of my wife. It doesn't matter how long we were married. It doesn't matter what caused her death. She was gone for the rest of my life. The shock of that reality caused a power outage.

A part of me was missing, a part I could never replace. The darkness every widow and widower knows descended on me. The depth of that darkness, filled with loneliness and sadness, can be experienced, but not imagined. I know that now, as do others who have lost a spouse.

But I still live, and it is necessary for me to fashion a different life for the time I have left. That is a given. I have choices to make. I can succumb to sadness and loneliness, sink deeper into the darkness, withdraw from everyone and everything familiar to me. Or I can set about the difficult business of beginning a journey on an unfamiliar trail and drawing the map along the way. Not for her, my family, my friends, important as they are, but for me.

I am still important. I have work to do, a map to draw for those who will inevitably take the same journey. I need to smile again, talk again, write again. We all have that which we must do or continue doing after the death of a spouse. So we do it. We are followers and leaders at the same time. Widows and widowers need empathetic models and companions. Few couples die together. One must always begin anew. So it is. Those beginning the journey are guided by others farther along the same trail, others who understand as only those on that trail can.

I am finding that my coin of grief, like other coins, has two sides. On the one side I am sad, lonely, scared. On the other side I am finding curiosity, anticipation, expectation. Something will happen, emerge, occur—something to relieve my pain, to give me hope, to make my journey one of healing and renewed energy. It will happen. I know that because I am still alive and all life has purpose and change.

Somehow, I will blend the past with the future and be a wiser person because I now know, acknowledge, and have experienced the impermanence of all living things, even those we loved the most. And on the other side of the coin, as I travel my new trail, I am learning how important it is to live while we are alive.

BUBBLES ON THE CEILING

I have been acquiring a lot of skills since becoming a single man, doing things that looked easy watching someone else do them. Anyone can do the laundry by instinct, right? Wrong! My instincts failed to inform me that after the dirty clothes are washed they need to go through a spin cycle before transferring them to the dryer. I am still mopping up puddles, and the dryer developed a hernia trying to do its job. I have learned that wearing damp socks and other close-to-the body apparel is more uncomfortable than wearing none at all.

I also learned that using half a bottle of dish-washing soap is too much for a small dishpan of dirty dishes. I have a kitchen ceiling decorated with soap bubbles that pop and leave wet spots on the floor.

How could I know that using paper towels as napkins for company is low on the social register and that mixed nuts are classier than peanuts in shells for cocktail parties, even if you are serving cheap wine? And what's wrong with serving wine in a beer glass? You get a bigger serving.

Plants need watering. Nothing lasts forever in the refrigerator. After several days there is no space to walk if you hang your clothes on the floor. It's a good idea to shave before going to a party. Every day, I am adding good ideas like that to my *don't forget to do* list.

Most difficult of all is making a bed. Nothing comes out even. And sheets have a sneaky way of making their way from the bottom of the bed to your neck while you are sleeping. I don't dare remove the bedspread. I would never get it on straight again. So now I just quietly slip into the bed by unfolding the tiniest piece of bedding and tuck any protruding bedding back in every morning. I do have one night every two weeks I sleep in a well-made bed. My housekeeper changes the bed every other Tuesday and remakes it with clean sheets. I have no idea how to fold when I put them out for her to find. So every other Tuesday I sleep like a baby in a well-made bed.

So there you have it. I have a lot of formal education with degrees and everything, but I still have a lot to learn. At this time in my new schooling it is still easier for me to write about making a bed than it is for me to make one.

THE LOAD LIGHTENS

Grief is a terrible companion. It weakens your knees, takes away your desire to live, and robs you of capabilities you thought could never be stolen from you.

It's a deep, dark pit with slippery sides and no steps to sunlight. Grief manifests itself in different ways for different grievers. Insomnia, loss of appetite, reclusiveness, fits of weeping, anger, fear can all be manifestations of grief.

As we grow older we have more reasons to grieve than when we were younger. We lose spouses, sometimes children, friends, and neighbors. Finding an obituary of someone we know in the newspaper becomes commonplace. Our own mental and physical strengths weaken. More and more we discover we cannot do what we once did easily.

We have our share of grieving neighbors at Westminster. We need to understand their changes in behavior, offer them comfort, listen to them talk, touch them when they need a touch. Those of us who are recovering from grief need to assure them, as I was assured, that the load grief presses upon us grows lighter with time. It does. One of the manifestations of my grief was the inability to concentrate for a long period of time. I couldn't read a book, watch a movie, sit through a concert. My life had to be broken into small segments. Short lunches were better than long dinners.

Now I am reading a book; I have watched a movie and seen a stage play from beginning to end. I can talk coherently about what once was and without visible emotion. I write this to give comfort and hope to those who must recover from the initial devastation of grief. It is true, as I was told, the load gets lighter with time, support from others, and the effort to stay connected to life.

HOME TO STAY

Perhaps some people can, but I can't—go back. My personal clock does not have a backward setting. My past is indeed my past. It is pleasant for me to think about places I have lived, houses I have lived in, once my homes. I enjoy talking about cars I have driven, jobs I have held. They are good memories, but I don't want them back. I am content and happy with what I have, where I am, and who I am, all different from what I had, where I was, and who I was. I will never resettle in a city I once called "home." That reality was clarified on a trip to a city I returned to recently.

My family and I returned to northern Wisconsin for my deceased wife's burial, where I will be buried when it is my time to join her. We both were born and raised and spent our professional lives there. We lived and worked in various cities and at those times called them "home." I left each one somewhat reluctantly and thought seriously about returning to one I especially enjoyed for my final years. I know now I cannot go back home, because I am home.

One of our grandsons asked me, "Grandpa, how does it feel to be home again?"

He knew how much I enjoyed living in that city and had spoken of someday returning to live there. His question startled me. I was momentarily disoriented.

The city had not changed much since I left, but apparently I had.

"This isn't home for me anymore, Alex," I answered. "When I leave tomorrow, I will be headed home." I don't know if he understood. Perhaps at the time I didn't. But saying that felt good.

I must have meant it. I am capable of returning to former homes, but I am not the same and, therefore, they wouldn't be either. I don't want to go back.

Now my home is here, as a resident of Westminster Community in Bradenton, Florida. I am comfortable, contented, and happy. I am a canoeist who has no desire to paddle upstream. I have reached a destination I can call "home." Until someone paddles me back to the place I once called "home," I will stay here for the remainder of my old age. And it feels good to write that.

CLOVER AND KEY

I held my sweet Mary 'till the moment she died.
She had given me sunshine, blue skies and pride.
But then came the dark clouds, the thunder and rain.
I was glad when it ended. God relieved her of pain.
I thought when she died my life was over.
But God found and sent me a four-leaf clover.
A clover named Rose came into my life.
She had some years before been another man's wife.
Now a widow, she was wary of me,
But God in His kindness sent her a key,
The key to open my lonely, old heart.
It beat once again, and got her heart to start.
So now we're together, Rosie and I,
Living with sunshine and mostly blue sky.
I can't forget Mary, would not if I could.
But life with Rosie is pretty darn good.
I know she thinks often of her other life,
The years she spent as another man's wife.
And I still cherish Mary, the life we two had.
We walked hand in hand through the good and the bad.
But we're alive again, Rosie and me:
And grateful to God for that clover and key.

PART FIVE

Lester

The storm was typical of those that follow ninety-degree, sultry summer days in central Wisconsin. The wind shook the tree tops, rain pelted the house, lightning flashed, thunder cracked, and even a few hailstones fell.

When the storm had blown itself eastward, we ventured outside to survey the damage. Our property had fared well, but two baby birds had not. The storm had blown them out of their nest, and their naked bodies lay panting for life on the cool wet grass under the oak tree from which they had fallen. They had already attracted a line of red ants when we found them. The one was too near dead to be revived. The other was searching with outstretched neck and open beak for its mother. We buried the first and carried the second inside in a shoe box.

The baby was either a robin or a blue jay, we thought. And neighbors who peered into the shoe box were pretty evenly divided on their guesses. It turned out that those who guessed robin were proved right when Lester began to sprout orange-gray fluff.

We fed Lester scrambled eggs and bait worms from Prizl's Corner Market. The robin had a good appetite and was soon gobbling bugs and small grasshoppers from our fingers in addition to his (her?) staples of eggs and worms.

We learned a lot about the growth and development of robins by parenting Lester. He loved his eggs, but he was chirpier after gulping creatures that had some wiggle left in them. And although the sides of his box were too high, he tried instinctively not to dirty his nest. It took much longer for him to grow feathers than we thought, but grow feathers he did; and he soon graduated from his shoe box to a plastic clothes basket with sides he could see through. He watched the world through his basket and pleaded for food whenever we touched the basket or even came near.

Lester chirped and fluttered in his basket during the daylight hours, but at night he remained still and quiet on the piece of wood we gave him for a perch. We felt a kind of affection passing between ourselves and the bird as we watched him grow. One day we found him perched on the rim of his basket with a belly full of scrambled eggs and worms, and we knew it was time for Lester to be out of his basket and outdoors, at least for some of the day. So we placed him in the shade on the ground near the house where we watched him hop a little, chirp a lot, and occasionally try to catch a passing ant. Every hour or so he showed up at the door asking for his eggs and worms. At dusk he was always at the door, ready to be put in his basket for the night.

Day by day Lester grew and spouted feathers that left no doubt as to his biological parentage. He was indeed a robin. Each day he hopped a little farther from the house, but quickly returned when one of us sang, "Little bird, little bird, in a cinnamon tree . . ." More and more successfully, he hunted ants and bugs and became less interested in scrambled eggs. One day he resisted eating from our fingers, and by cocking his head he told us to drop whatever we were serving at his feet where he eyed it suspiciously before snapping it up. Lester was clearly displaying the emerging independence of adolescence.

He began a hop-fly kind of locomotion as he moved between destinations more than a few yards apart. We rejoiced in this growth spurt much as parents watching a child's first steps would. His feathers were not fully grown, but Lester could fly, at least a little.

We wanted more from our bird; so we perched him on a tree branch about five feet from the ground, stepped back, and sang our little-bird song. After an hour of intermittent singing with no movement from Lester, we returned him to the ground.

We repeated his flight training every day, and within a week Lester was hopping from branch to branch in one of our small oak trees. We introduced him to a white pine and then another, and within a week Lester felt at home in three or four small trees in our large yard. But he refused to fly to us from his trees regardless of how often, how loudly, how on-key, how off-key we sang his song. Lester was clearly exhibiting teenage behavior. He would have his way in spite of our obvious wishes. If he were in school, we estimated, his reluctance to please his teachers would put him somewhere near the seventh grade.

In his trees, Lester made no attempt to search for food; so we fed him from our fingers, dropping scrambled eggs and worms into his outstretched beak. When we stopped feeding him in his trees and stood back with his plate of eggs and box of worms in sight, he flew to us quickly. Our robin had soloed at last.

Day by day Lester flew higher and farther. From pine tree, to oak tree, to house roof, to garage roof, and to us when we called. We held him, perched him on our heads, and stroked his feathers. So did our grandchildren. But Lester was most at ease with his mom and pop. We were sure he thought he looked like us.

We slept very little the first night we left him outdoors. At six in the morning we spotted him on the roof of the house, watching the sunrise and waiting for his breakfast. Lester was now a big boy (girl?). He could stay out all night.

We took our robin with us to visit friends and relatives. Neighbors brought their kids and grandkids to see him and to watch us feed him. When we walked between the house and the garage, he flew from roof to roof. We knew he was too attached to us and we to him because fall was in the air, and Lester soon had to be ready to travel with birds of his own feather.

We tried to force a separation by carrying him down our long path to the lake and leaving him there. But whenever we appeared to check on his wellbeing, he quickly appeared from wherever, asking to be fed. And we fed him, which was a mistake because he began meeting us on the path closer and closer to the house until one morning we found him once again watching the sunrise from the roof of the house and waiting for his eggs and worms.

Lester became less and less interested in being fed by us. We observed that he was becoming a better hunter, and we surmised that being fed by us was more a habit than a necessity for him. Maybe he was eating our offerings to be polite. At any rate, he ate less of the food we dropped at his feet.

One evening we saw Lester on a telephone wire about a mile down the road. We knew it was he because of his recognizable chirp and the crooked feather neither he nor we seemed able to straighten. We were happy he was expanding his territory, and we hoped he would find other robins to flock with.

Indeed, the robins around our lake were beginning to flock for migration. We too were beginning preparations for our return to Florida for the fall and winter months. Knowing he could never survive a Wisconsin winter alone, we worried that Lester might get left behind by the other robins.

Our worries heightened when we noted Lester's tendency to seek us out more often and stay closer to home. It seemed he was always making contact with us, even to the point of flying to the car as we drove in the driveway. He was obviously watching us more closely. We conjectured that he didn't want to be left behind when we migrated, assuming that we had the same instincts as he—not an entirely incorrect assumption.

Our departure for the South was only three weeks away. We had decided to pack Lester in a cage of some kind and take him with us—legal or not. We joked about ordering for him at restaurants along our route and how he would supply our wakeup calls in motel rooms. We debated about the best state for our boy (girl?) to winter in and decided on Alabama. Many urged us to take him all the way to our Florida home, but there are no freshwater lakes or ponds on our small island. So Alabama it was to be.

We arranged a final visit to Marinette, some 150 miles northeast, to say goodbye to family there, and told Lester to mind the house while we were gone. "And find some friends to fly south with," we added, quite sure that he would not.

We were wrong. When we returned after an overnight in Marinette, Lester was gone. We sang, whistled, and called with egg plate and worm box in hand. We walked the path to the lake and back a dozen times. We queried our neighbors. But Lester was gone. Our joy and sadness were hard to reconcile. We recalled Wordsworth's *Lines Written in Early Spring*.

> I heard a thousand blended notes,
> While in a grove I sat reclined.
> In that sweet mood when pleasant thoughts,
> Bring sad thoughts to the mind.

And Shelley's *To a Skylark,*

Hail to thee, blithe spirit!
Bird thou never wert,
That from heaven, or near it,
Pourest thy full heart,
In profuse strains of unpremeditated art.

Lester was gone, and so was a little bit of ourselves. He was probably only a robin and not an angel as we joked and sometimes felt. But his joyful presence was in a way an angelic ministration that calmed and gave hope in a world that seems to stray farther and farther from a natural plan.

Few birds have generated as much interest in their migrations as Lester, the robin we raised the summer of '94 and hoped would return to our Wisconsin retreat the summer of '95.

We told the story of Lester's fall from his oak tree nest and of his growth and development while in our care to family, friends, and even strangers with whom we shared checkout lines at Albertson's and Walmart. Many shared a tale of their own about a robin who returned summer after summer to the place of its hatching. And nearly all assured us Lester would be back. "He'll be back," they said. "Wait and see."

Only Norman, our summer neighbor and winter caretaker, thought otherwise. His eighty years of rural living told him Lester was dead. "He was too civilized," he said, "and he had a crooked feather. No way he could keep up with the flock. A cat probably got him."

Indeed, Lester was very civilized for a wild bird. He preferred our company to the company of other robins, and he did have a feather neither he nor we seemed able to straighten. But surely he was able to fly south with his natural kinfolk and elude cats along the route, or so we told ourselves.

We thought, talked, and joked about Lester often during our

winter months in Florida. We speculated as to his whereabouts and scrutinized the wing feathers of every robin that hopped into the neighborhood. We even drank toasts, "To Lester, wherever he may be!" at cocktail parties. Those who knew his story had unofficially banded together as a Friends of Lester Society. We all hoped he would find a female in a nest in that oak tree to welcome him home. "There will be little Lesters hopping all over the place," Ralph predicted.

The winter months passed, and in May our own migratory instincts kicked in. We left Perico Bay Club wondering if Lester would be waiting for us on the garage roof, one of his favorite perches, when we drove into the driveway back home. We also wondered where the currents in our life stream would carry us the next several months. From experience we knew the unexpected is inevitable and the next segment of our own migratory circle would not be uneventful. We would not be the same birds who left our Perico Bay Club nest when we returned in the fall.

Illinois is a long, dreary drive, and we drive from bottom to top on our trip north. This year the trip was somewhat less tedious because of the anticipation of seeing Lester soon. We speculated fancifully, "Who knows, Lester may be flying right above us. Unlikely, but who knows?" We exited Illinois 51 at Rockford, which is just a flap and a flutter away from the Wisconsin border, in good spirits.

With each mile we became more certain that Lester too was nearing his birthplace. "How will we recognize him?" I asked. "After all, don't all robins look pretty much alike? What if he doesn't have a crooked feather anymore? Will he come to our call as he did before we left? What if we take up with the wrong bird?" Nonsense, we concluded—parents never mistake their kids, and vice-versa. We would recognize Lester, okay, and he would remember us. We were sure of that, quite sure as we sped northward.

When we pulled into our driveway, we looked expectantly as the garage roof. No bird of any kind. A quick survey of the grounds around the buildings turned up nothing. There were no birds in the area, a discomfiting omen.

We unlocked the house door, stepped inside, and felt the familiarity of the place. The water pump was shocked into service after an eight-month rest, the car was unpacked, every room briefly looked into, and the telephones tested for dial tones. Our migration was completed. We were back. But was Lester back also? we wondered, no longer as certain of his return as we had been driving through Illinois.

After testing our favorite chairs and assuring each other it was good to be up north again, we checked the yard from the windows on all sides of the house. We saw a rabbit, a squirrel, and a bluejay, but no robins. "Maybe it's too early for robins to be back," I said, knowing full well that was nonsense.

In a telephone conversation a week earlier with Pete Lohr, longtime friend and now down-the-road neighbor, he had described a robin he saw on our lake path. "Healthy-looking," he said, "and tamer than most. Hopped the path just ahead of us quite a ways. Seemed friendly. Could be Lester."

Together we again peered through the windows. No birds. We moved outside and sang, "Little bird, little bird . . ." The melody that had brought Lester hopping eight months earlier sent a chipmunk under the picnic table on the patio scampering away, but attracted no birds. So we made the trek to the lake and back, singing all the way. We frightened a few rabbits and chickadees, even flushed a grouse, but no robins showed up.

Inside the house again we noticed dirt smudges outside of the dining room and bedroom windows, above the boxes that would soon be planted with our traditional pink petunias. We went outside to investigate and found bird droppings on the ground under the boxes. And the dirt in the boxes was disturbed and littered with dry grass and twigs. We also noticed the beginnings of a bird nest behind the porch light next to the front door. Clearly, a bird of some kind had been trying to take up residence in our absence, a trespasser with feathers and maybe an orange breast.

The next morning Norman walked over to welcome us back. He walked a little slower than he did when he walked over to say good-bye eight months earlier. I wondered if eight months when you're eighty is the same as eight months when you're sixty-five. I guessed not. He looked fit, however, and his powers of observation were sharp as ever.

"Big robin trying to get in your house for two weeks," he reported. "Looks at his reflection in your windows and tries to chase the bird he sees away. Chases other birds that come around the place away, too." He paused. "But they all do that this time of year," he went on hesitantly, "staking out their claims."

Perhaps even Norman was revising his faith in Lester's return.

We, at this point, were sure Lester was back. We had a robin trying to break into our house, probably the same one building a nest behind the front porch light. And Pete Lohr had seen a tame robin on our lake path. It had to be Lester. Why not? Made sense. Our boy (or girl) had come home as we had. Perico Bay Club seemed long ago and far away.

"But we haven't seen any robins yet," we told Norman.

"They flew north to get away from you Southerners. Ain't goin' to come around now that you're here."

Norman had always considered our Florida move an act of disloyalty. The Florida license plate on the rear bumper of our car was a real test of friendship. But, like my parents, he was sure our fit would pass, and we would regain our senses and abandon our winter jaunts away from the great state of Wisconsin. Interestingly, research into the replacements of retirees shows that more snowbirds return to their original home states for their final years than live out their lives in the South. "The best laid plans of mice and men" I guess.

Norman said he had placed a barrier on our electric meter box near our patio doors at the back of the house. "A robin keeps building a nest there. I knocked it down a dozen times, but the bird won't give up. I got a piece of plywood leaning over the box against the house."

A nest on our meter box was not unusual. Nearly every spring a robin builds a nest on that box, lays her eggs, and then abandons the nest because of the traffic in and out of the nearby doors. So to spare the poor birds the trauma that must come from nest abandonment, we try to knock the nests down before they are fully constructed, an example of being cruel to be kind.

We walked to the rear of the house and viewed Norman's dissuader. No one could fault his creativity. The bird hasn't been hatched that could build a nest on a piece of plywood leaning against a house. But we did wonder if this year we were doing the right thing. After all, the bird in question just might be Lester or Mrs. Lester.

"Good work, Norman," I said without complete conviction.

The next two days were given to opening the buildings, grocery shopping, making lists of things to do this summer, and watching a robin watch us from his or her perch on one or the other of our window boxes. However, he (she?) always flew away before we got near enough to the window for a feather check. We also watched the painful maneuvers of the same, or different, robin trying to build a nest under the plywood covering of the electric meter box. Of course, it was an impossible undertaking, but this bird seemed to ignore that reality. The grass and twigs it carried to the plywood and tried to tuck under it fell uselessly to the ground, but the bird remained undaunted and always escaped our view before we could get a good look at its feathers. We also watched the garage roof closely for any bird sign, without luck.

On the third day after our return we headed the Buick northward again to visit my parents, who had assured us all winter by telephone and letter that they were doing just fine. "Don't worry about us up here in the cold," they comforted. "We're used to the ice and snow." But we worried anyway—needlessly, it seemed, because they were indeed doing just fine when we arrived.

After the usual greetings had been exchanged, they asked about Lester, whom they had first met in his clothes basket and who had hopped around their backyard on a previous visit. At that time, they predicted he would return the following summer and were now eager to know if he had.

"We think he's back," we told them, and laid out the evidence we had. They agreed the evidence was compelling and that he must be back.

"If he's smart," my dad said, "he'll stay up here instead of going back to all that heat and humidity." Like Norman, my parents couldn't understand our move to Florida. They wished we would stay where we belonged.

Two days with my parents passed quickly, and we reversed our engines for the return trip to the lake, southward again. "We're going in circles," I commented. And it occurred to me that life itself is like a big circle. We are born, arc our ways across the years, and as Shakespeare points out, exit the stage much the same way we entered, "in second childishness, and mere oblivion, sans teeth, sans eyes, sans taste, sans everything," our circles completed.

The trip home passed quickly. With eyes focused on the garage roof, now an obsession, we pulled into our driveway. The roof was still bare. "I think we're engaging in wishful thinking," I suggested. "Lester's not going to show up again." Just then, a pair of robins flew out of the oak tree from which Lester had been blown a year ago, and we thought we saw a crooked feather on the wing of the larger of the two. We couldn't be sure, but our optimism returned.

The next day, thinking the nest building was over, I removed the plywood from the electric meter and made a mental note to return it to Norman who had a use for everything. There were many robins around our place now, but none seemed to be building a nest. Besides, the area around the electric meter was free of debris, a sure sign, I thought, that Norman had managed to discourage the most determined bird in Adams County. And since our watching and singing had given us nothing definite to pin our hopes on, we had little reason to believe we would ever know if Lester truly had returned. If he had, we concluded, he had forgotten us and was with a mate in the oak tree out front, a happy ending in itself. And on that note we left to spend a few days in Minneapolis.

When we returned from Minneapolis, we were surprised to find a robin's nest on the electric meter we had shielded so diligently. In the nest was one small, blue egg. I immediately reported our find to Norman. "There'll be three more in there," he said. "They always lay four eggs." The next day there were two more eggs in the nest. The fourth never did appear. Even Norman makes mistakes.

Soon a female robin was on the nest, skittish as any bird would be nesting arm's length from a busy doorway. "Like trying to take a nap on an I-75 exit ramp," I observed. "Serves her right." However, we avoided the back door as much as possible and entertained the notion that somehow Lester was implicated in this example of poor judgement. We never did believe it was Lester on the nest. The bird on the nest was too ill-tempered and nervous to be our kin. Birds do have personalities of a sort, and this bird was definitely not one of us. She left the nest at the slightest provocation and stayed away most of the day. We worried about the condition of her eggs. If she were Lester's bride, we didn't approve of his selection.

One morning I was sitting at my desk under a window facing the garage. It was a cool, sunny blue-sky morning. The tall, skinny jack pines that sway in the slightest breeze were motionless, but the squirrels and chipmunks that scampered up and down them were not. The woodland creatures were up and out early that morning. I had also seen several rabbits sniffing their way around the garage and a doe heading toward the lake, probably thirsty from an early-morning treat at Norman's saltlick.

Out of habit I glanced at the garage roof. There, in Lester's favorite early-morning perch, was a male robin. He stood as still as the jack pines that framed him in the pinkish-yellow rays of the nearly-risen sun. What a beauty he was with his head high and his sleek, orange breast catching the morning light. This was a bird without humility, a bird with an air of elegance, a confident bird, a bird who had flown south and returned safely. It had to be Lester.

I leaned closer to the window to get a better look at his wing feathers. He cocked his head in my direction. The bird was watching me as I was watching him. I was sure of that.

We stared at each other for more than a minute. I thought of getting the binoculars, but I feared I might lose him if I broke eye contact. Try as I did, I could not get a good look at his feathers.

The window in the adjoining room faced the garage at a slightly different angle. Would he stay put if I disappeared for a moment? I decided to risk it and dashed for the bedroom next door. He had not moved, but my angle of vision was still wrong. And now I couldn't be certain that he saw me. I waited and watched. Perhaps the robin would change his position. I really needed to know if the bird on the garage roof had a crooked feather, but he didn't seem about to cooperate by turning sideways.

Should I leave my post and go outside for a better look? Would he leave his perch if I made the move? As I deliberated, the bird lowered his head, opened his wings and half glided, half fluttered from the roof, past my window and toward the front porch where we had so often fed Lester his scrambled eggs and worms.

I whirled and headed for the kitchen window that looked out on the porch. "Let him be there," I whispered, and my request was granted. He was there, head cocked toward the door, his back to my window, his crooked feather protruding from an otherwise sleek, tidy plumage. It was Lester, all right. How many robins with crooked feathers came to my front door? He quickly made a half turn, now facing me, orange breast forward. And just as quickly, he left the porch and flew into the branches of a nearby white pine where he was hidden from my view.

I wished he had given me a better look. The glimpse I had was too brief. I tried to conjure up a mental picture of the bird with his back to me. I tried to see again, in my mind, that crooked feather. I was both sure and unsure that I had seen it.

Suddenly it occurred to me that the bird on the porch was asking to be fed. Lester had apparently seen me watching him on the garage roof. My image had triggered something in his brain, and he had instinctively associated me with food. I needed some scrambled eggs and worms in a hurry, to lure him back so I could have another look. But I had none.

So I found Lester's old plate and carried it empty to the front porch. Half shielding the plate to hide its emptiness I held it shoulder high and sang, "Little bird, little bird." No response. I walked to the white pine and repeated the performance. I could hear and see some branch movement, but no bird emerged. In desperation, I foolishly slid the plate into the branches. A bird flew out the other side of the tree and across the road, too fast for me to see anything but a blur. I returned to the house.

A day or two later we observed two heads bobbing out of the nest on the electric meter, perhaps Lester's offspring. Their mother seemed to us less attentive than she should have been, but the babies grew larger each day. They begged for food with their beaks apart and searching as Lester had when he was in our care. We watched closely and believed only one bird, their mother, was feeding them. If Lester were their father, he obviously felt his job was over.

We watched the babies grow from a distance, and used our patio doors as little as possible. One day we noticed the nest was empty. After a few days I decided the nest had been abandoned. I got out the ladder and looked inside it. One small, blue egg, the third, lay there unhatched.

I removed the egg, walked a few paces into the woods and buried it in some tall grasses. I placed the nest on the woodpile behind the garage. For some reason it didn't seem right to take it far from the house.

Lester never appeared again. That is, we saw no more robins acting unusually or familiarly. But we think Lester spent the summer with us and made contact in the only way he knew how. We may never see him again, another chapter, another circle, and so it goes.

Then again, we may see him next summer, or the next or the next. We'll be watching for him. And perhaps he'll be waiting for us as we, like the other creatures on our planet, and indeed our planet itself, circle our ways through the seasons and the years.

ACKNOWLEDGMENTS

I would like to acknowledge Carole Sanders, who was editor of the *Echo* and the *Writer's Quarterly* when I wrote the selections in this book. She encouraged me to write for an older population and always assured me that what I wrote was being well received. I thank her for writing the foreword for this book. I would also like to thank the residents and staff of Westminster Retirement Community at Bradenton, Florida. They gave me subject matter to write about and praised what I wrote. Roy and Jo Williams read my stuff and encouraged me to write on the topics I did. They are residents of a neighboring retirement community. The marketing department for our Westminster community sent copies of our publications to prospective residents and shared positive comments from those prospective residents with me. All in all, I probably would not have published this book were it not for the encouragement I had along the way. And Koehler Books, which was as supportive of these musings as they were with the previous two books of mine they published.

ABOUT THE AUTHOR

DR. RICHARD J. SMITH is Professor Emeritus, University of Wisconsin, Madison, and recipient of a Distinguished Teaching Award from that university. His major emphases of study were the development of reading comprehension and the development of positive attitudes toward reading. His research and classroom practice determined that reading can be a springboard to higher-level thinking behaviors that increase reading pleasure.

Professor Smith is author or co-author of five college textbooks on the teaching of reading and numerous instructional materials for the development of reading as a thinking process. In addition, he has published more than fifty articles in professional journals for teachers of reading and reading researchers.

His professional career included classroom teaching, Director for Reading Development for the Madison, Wisconsin Schools and consultant to school districts at the national level.

Since his retirement in 1990, Professor Smith has written numerous short stories and published two books, *Life After Eighty* and *Once Upon a Christmas*. The prose and poetry in this book were written during the four years he has resided in the Bradenton, Florida, Westminster Retirement Community, and were published in the two publications for residents of that community.